YOU
HAVE A
CHOICE

Paperback Edition

Creative Director: Saeah Wood
Production & Editorial Manager: Amy Reed
Editorial: Amy Reed & Christa Evans
Design: Ivica Jandrijević

Grateful acknowledgment is made for permission to reprint the following:
Page 120: "How it Works" comic by Randall Munro/xkcd (https://xkcd.
com/385/) is licensed under Creative Commons BY-NC 2.5.

Paperback: 979-8-9890941-0-3
E-Book: 979-8-9890941-1-0

otterpine.com

ERIC NEHRLICH

YOU
HAVE A
CHOICE

Beyond Hard Work to Meaningful Impact

For each of you who helped me to
discover and choose my own path

Contents

3. ACCEPT YOUR PARTS

4. ACCEPT OTHERS

5. EXPERIMENT AND LEARN

6. ADDRESS THE BLOCKERS

7. PAY ATTENTION

8. ASPIRE

Introduction

How do you feel about your life?

If you love it, this book isn't for you. Keep doing what you're doing.

If not, does the following resonate?

From the outside, you seem like you have it figured out. You're on a career track that other people dream of, with a job you worked hard to get, at a company that excited you when you first joined. This feels like it should be your happily ever after, yet you're not satisfied.

Despite the external validation, you feel exhausted and drained at the end of each day. Your life is an endless stream of tasks and emails and meetings, with no way to get it all done. It feels like a game of Tetris—each time you go up a level, the game speeds up and sends more at you, and eventually you will drown in pieces and lose.

But losing is not an option. The work still needs to get done. You know how to do the work, and your boss and team are depending on you. So you keep going, one long day at a time.

You dream of a change, of something different—but what? You come up with ideas, but they all sound impossibly unrealistic. You're tired of feeling this way, but you don't see how you can change your life without everything falling apart.

I used to be you. I spent my whole life exceeding expectations, getting straight As so I could get into a top university, then building my skills at several startup jobs before getting the opportunity to work at Google. I was trusted with such important responsibilities that I was regularly in meetings with the top executives at Google, and I felt determined to deliver because I was not going to waste this opportunity. But a couple years later, I was working from 8:00 a.m. to midnight every day including most weekends, drowning in emails and meetings and tasks, and feeling miserable and disillusioned.

Now, my work is meaningful and inspiring to me, and I work when I choose. I spend quality time with my family, while still having time for my own pursuits like writing this book. I am designing my own life, day by day, to create impact that aligns with my values.

What changed?

I realized I had been letting other people run my life: my parents, my managers, my coworkers, my friends, even random people I had just met. I had set myself the impossible task of keeping everyone around me happy by always delivering above their expectations.

And I also realized I had a choice: I could keep going as I had been, letting my success be defined by the expectations of others. Or I could find a new path, one where I choose my own definition of success.

As part of redesigning my life, I became an executive coach so I could help leaders grow their impact by sharing with them the principles and mindsets I had used to change my own life. I wrote this book to share those ideas more broadly; I want you to do more than survive each week, and instead start on a journey of discovery to create a more meaningful life for yourself.

The advice in this book is simple to understand, but not necessarily easy to follow. We all know we should eat healthy and exercise, but how many of us do it? I tell my clients that nothing will change just because we talk—they need to do something different with what they learn. The same applies to the advice I share in this book: nothing will happen because you read this book unless you do something different with what you read.

Your life will change when you change your life. By sharing what has worked for me and my clients, I hope that you will take a look at your current life with fresh eyes and feel empowered to try just one experiment to change things. That's the moment that can change everything.

Once you realize that you have the power to make a different choice, you will start to see even more choices to create new possibilities. And as you keep making new choices, you may find yourself creating a life that is unimaginable from where you are today.

This approach worked for me, it has worked for the many successful leaders I have coached, and it will work for you—if you are willing to embrace the process and do the work.

Let's start with the key principles that will guide you in this journey.

The only thing you control is your next action

You can't change the past. It's already happened, and nothing you do will change that. If you don't like what happened, you can avoid responsibility by looking for somebody to blame, or make other excuses. You can spend hours beating yourself up and wishing you had done things differently. But to get different results, you must learn from what happened and take different actions going forward.

You can't control the future. The world is too uncertain and complex for you to ensure that you get the future you want, no matter how carefully you plan. I had great plans for how 2020 would unfold for my coaching business, and the COVID-19 pandemic upended all of them. And now that I'm a parent of two young kids, I am learning to hold my plans even more lightly.

You can't control others. You can try to influence and persuade them, but they choose their actions, not you. What they do is frequently a response to their own experiences, rather than having anything to do with you.

If you can't change the past or the future, and you can't control others, what's left is the present moment and yourself. What you *can* control is choosing your next action with purpose. In other words...

You have a choice

With that control comes the responsibility to intentionally choose your actions. This includes the stories you tell yourself about the events that happen around you, which affects how you react to those events.

You can give that responsibility to others. Instead of choosing what you do, you can let your manager choose, or your parents, or your friends, or your community. These others may not even have to tell you what they want, as you may have internalized their expectations (or your assumptions about their expectations) as nagging voices in your head on constant repeat.

But giving that responsibility to others means you have given away the one thing you control, which is why you feel helpless and stuck. Every time something happens, you have a choice about how to respond: you can react the way you previously have, which will likely get the same results, or you can choose a new option that might lead to different possibilities. Your freedom comes from taking the responsibility to make that choice.

I'm not saying your choices will be easy. There can be difficult consequences, and your past choices may constrain you in real and unfortunate ways. If you stretch financially to buy a house that is beyond your means and the economy enters a downturn, that mortgage will constrain your actions: you might have to stay in a job you hate because it's well paying and stable, or if you choose to leave, it might affect your ability to keep the house. There's no easy choice in this situation, but that doesn't mean you can't leave your job—you just can't leave your job *and* keep paying the mortgage.

I once burned out so badly at Google that I had a 103-degree fever on Christmas Day and was sick for a week. I had been working 100+ hour weeks for months because I wanted to prove I deserved a promotion by delivering stellar results on all of the work my manager gave to me. But lying in bed that week, I asked myself whether that promotion was worth sacrificing my health, my happiness, and my time with my friends and family.

That was my epiphany moment when I first realized I had a choice. I had spent my whole life believing I had to exceed the expectations of others (my parents, teachers, managers, and coworkers) to earn love and acceptance. If I didn't deliver successfully on a task, I risked the unimaginable consequence of being seen as a failure. But that manager was giving me more work than I could handle, and it was destroying me.

I had never previously turned down a challenge because I was terrified of what might happen if I admitted I couldn't do something. But I could no longer accept the damage that was being done to my mental and physical health and my relationships. I decided that I no longer wanted to continue working as I had been, and I was ready to face the potential consequences and quit if things didn't change. I shared that decision with my manager when I came back to work in January.

Even though I didn't get fired, that choice still had consequences. My manager told me that if I couldn't handle the work, they would give it to somebody who could, and they took away half my team. They also slashed my performance rating from "strongly exceeds expectations" to "barely meets expectations," which meant I lost any chance at that promotion. My worst fears had been realized, and I expected that it would mean the end of my world, as I had revealed myself as a failure with no value who couldn't handle my job.

But that's not what happened. Instead of the soul-crushing defeat I had feared, I felt an uplifting freedom. Rather than spending my evenings and weekends on work I found meaningless, I worked 40 hours a week for the same salary, and I invested the time that I got back into my health, my friends, and other activities meaningful to me. I had failed to meet the expectations of that manager, but I had chosen my well-being over Google, and that choice changed my life in ways that are still unfolding to this day.

You have a choice, too. You can choose how you spend your time in each moment and each day. You can choose how you show up in your interactions. I want you to have the same epiphany I had: you have more possibilities and choices available to you than you even realize. I hope you don't have to reach the same bottom I did to have it.

And once you see that you have a choice, you get to **choose what matters most to you in life**.

We rarely make such choices consciously or intentionally. We discover what works well for us as a child or in school, and then we keep doing that, because...

Change means letting go

Once you learn a set of behaviors that bring you success, you usually keep doing them even if your situation changes. That makes sense! Why change something that's working?

And yet these actions that previously brought success may be the exact set of behaviors that are now keeping you stuck. Navigating the next set of challenges requires letting go of what once worked for you and learning a new set of skills and actions.

The root cause of such limiting behaviors often lies in beliefs that you hold about yourself. Here are a few such limiting beliefs that I see both in myself and my clients:

- **I must solve problems myself.** If you ask for help, you fear that you will appear as if you're incompetent or don't know what you're doing. Figuring it out yourself leads to great success in school and early in one's career when performance is evaluated on an individual basis. However, as you take on more and bigger challenges, it can quickly lead to a state of overwhelm with all the problems you feel you have to solve yourself instead of relying on help from other people.

- **Working harder is the answer.** Children are rewarded for effort: you get credit for showing your work, and activities like sports and music teach you that more work leads to a proportional amount of success, i.e., if you practice more, you get better. So, you continue to apply that mental model in life because you believe that working harder will inevitably lead to proportional results. Unfortunately, the world is often nonlinear and nonintuitive,[1] so working harder on the wrong things is ineffective and may even reinforce the current situation. Rather than being the answer, working harder can lead to burnout, because the harder you work, the further you get behind.

- **I can't say no.** As children, we are taught that we must obey our teachers and other authority figures; doing so brings us success (and gold stars!), so we think we have to keep doing it to be successful. We fear that saying no to others may lead to hard conversations or rejection so we say yes to everything, taking on more and more commitments until we can no longer reliably deliver.

---

[1] Systems thinking explores these nonlinear effects. Two introductory books on the topic are *Thinking in Systems* by Donella Meadows (2008) and *The Fifth Discipline* by Peter Senge (1990).

You can see how the combination of those beliefs led to me burning out at Google. I couldn't say no to my manager, so I took on more and more work. I couldn't ask for help because I thought that would indicate that I couldn't handle my job. So I worked harder and harder and destroyed my health, rather than let go of those beliefs.

You might be holding on to similar beliefs that were effective for you when you first learned them, which makes them particularly difficult to let go of. Because they helped get you certain results, you may stop getting those results if you stop doing them, which may lead to a step back in performance. That won't feel good!

But that attachment to your current beliefs means you are also stuck at your current level of performance; reaching the next level requires letting go of those beliefs, and learning new ones. Taking a step back may mean a short-term decline in performance, but experimenting with new behaviors can set you up for a giant step forward.[2]

Again, you have a choice. It may not seem like a *good* choice right now, because you've spent your whole life on a linear path where your performance is always improving, and any decline or detour from that path feels like a failure. But learning new skills means pushing through the discomfort of being an unskilled beginner. Will you choose to experience that discomfort if it can unlock a potential leap in your performance?

These examples illustrate that while we may want to blame others for our situation (our parents, our managers, the expectations of others), we still have a choice as to what actions we take. If we do not see those choices, and/or choose not to make different choices,

---

[2] Jerry Weinberg (1986) has a wonderful illustration of this in his book *Becoming a Technical Leader*, where he writes that we think growth looks a steady, linear, up-and-to-the-right increase, but instead it looks like a set of plateaus: we learn a new set of skills, plateau in performance, then have to let go of those skills and take a step back in performance to learn a new set of skills for reaching the next plateau. It never feels "right" to do worse, but our unwillingness to let go of our current performance level is what keeps us stuck on a plateau.

then we are responsible for the consequences. Our refusal to let go of our current beliefs is the reason our situation is not changing, which leads to this question:

How are you the problem?

This question is not meant to shame or blame you for everything that you dislike in your life. It is meant to remind you of the agency you have to create your life and to help you take responsibility for the choices you make.

When you feel stuck, this book will help you understand the ways you might be contributing to that stuckness through your unwillingness to let go of your expectations of yourself or others, commitments you've previously made, or an identity that no longer serves you.

Privilege check: I am not saying you are the only problem. I write this as a white-passing man in America, who was brought up with financial security and abundant educational options. I recognize that my privilege has sheltered me from having to face external obstacles,[3] so in this book I am more focused on the internal obstacles. I believe these principles apply regardless of your relative privilege, as similar concepts are cited by authors such as Shellye Archambeau (2020) and Arlan Hamilton (2020). But I am not the right person to write about how to face structural racism, economic inequality, or systemic oppression. This book is designed for people who are the main contributors to keeping themselves stuck and have the capacity to do something about it.

---

[3] I share some reflections on how my privilege helped me at various points in my life at https://toomanytrees.substack.com/p/juneteenth.

Once you recognize that you are part of the problem, you have a choice:

1. You can keep doing what you're doing and stay stuck,[4] or

2. You can change by letting go of your previous responses and start experimenting with different actions that might change the situation and get you unstuck.

As an example, most leaders know what they should do to be a more effective leader—they've read all the advice and have learned the best practices. But they're not doing them, because they are not willing to let go of previous behaviors.[5]

A CEO of a start-up once told me "I know I should delegate more, and I know I need to give this difficult feedback, but I just don't do it." He had built his career on solving problems himself by diving into the details and providing the answer. And that worked great when the company was 10 or even 20 people. But as the company grew to 30 people, then 40, he became the bottleneck. Rather than giving people feedback or coaching them on how to handle things, he just did it himself. As a result, every problem had to wait on him, because he had not learned to let go of solving problems himself and trust others to handle them.

For the company to keep growing, he had to let go of the thrill of being a superhero, swooping in to save the day. Instead, he had to build a team that could handle problems without him—which felt terrifying! He had thrived on feeling indispensable, as if the whole company rested on his shoulders. If people could do the

---

[4] Jerry Colonna, the executive coach known as the "CEO Whisperer", regularly asks: "How are you complicit in creating the circumstances you say you don't want?" It's not meant as a blaming question, but one that encourages you to reflect on how your actions contribute to the situation staying as it is.

[5] Robert Kegan and Lisa Lahey's book *Immunity to Change* (2009) describes this as an unconscious commitment to how we do things today that prevents us from changing to fulfill the conscious commitments we say we want.

work without him, what was his role? How would he add value? He unconsciously resisted the unpleasant path of answering those difficult questions and stuck to what he knew. But the pain of his situation grew until he realized that his unwillingness to change was the problem, and he chose to take on the discomfort of letting go of his current behaviors to start on a new path of growth.

How to use this book

In the rest of this book, I use the principles of "How are you the problem?" and "You have a choice" to guide you out of your dissatisfaction and create a more fulfilling life.

Throughout the book, I periodically pause to apply these two principles as a framework to demonstrate how to transform a perceived problem into a different choice you can make. I also illustrate these principles with stories from my clients as well as my own struggles around similar challenges.

To help you find your path, I offer reflection questions and exercises throughout each chapter. These questions and exercises are not meant to be glanced at and skimmed over; engaging with them will help you uncover new possibilities for yourself. In fact, each time you are stuck, you may come back to these exercises and repeat them to discover new ways in which you are unconsciously holding yourself back.

How you do these exercises is not important; you can write in a journal, type on a computer, or even dictate into a notes app. What matters is that you take the time to reflect on the questions and articulate your answers in some form that can be reviewed later. As I said earlier, your life will not change by reading this book unless you do the uncomfortable work of change, and it starts by answering the questions in these exercises.

Here's what you will find in the chapters ahead:[6]

Chapter 1: Aim—Start by picking a direction, an idea of how you want things to be different. We will also explore what might motivate you to start changing your life.

Chapter 2: Accept Yourself—Reflect on why you might be blocking yourself from the change you want. Understanding how and why you react as you do today will help you make more effective plans to change your life.

Chapter 3: Accept Your Parts—By understanding the different parts of your brain that want different things, you will be better equipped to navigate the conflicting and contradictory desires that "you" have. As you learn to consciously mediate between your various parts, you will find greater clarity and choose actions to align with that clarity.

Chapter 4: Accept Others—By accepting other people as they are, you will become more effective at working with and influencing them.

Chapter 5: Experiment and Learn—Once you have accepted the reality of yourself and others, you can experiment to learn what works and doesn't work to move your situation in your desired direction.

Chapter 6: Address the Blockers—This chapter offers tools to address several common patterns that block progress.

Chapter 7: Pay Attention—Staying on your chosen path requires paying attention to notice when and how you fall back into

---

[6] This approach is loosely inspired by the GROW coaching model, which is copyrighted by the Estate of Sir John Whitmore and Performance Consultants (n.d.):
- Goal (what do I want? aka Aim)
- Reality (what's my current reality? aka Accept)
- Options (what can I try from this reality? aka Experiment)
- Will (what will I do?)

It's a simple but effective model that helps people gain clarity on their situation and how to move forward.

previous behaviors. This chapter offers strategies to hold yourself accountable for letting go of what previously worked for you so you can stay on the uncomfortable—but ultimately rewarding—path of change and growth.

Chapter 8: Aspire—Once you have learned these skills of growth and change, you can think bigger. How will you change not only yourself, but the world around you?

This book is filled with ideas and practices designed to help you on your journey. Don't expect to absorb it all on the first read. These practices are easy to understand but difficult to do consistently because they require letting go of what previously worked for you. The process that I'm laying out in this book is designed to be repeatable. You will find yourself stuck or unsatisfied in different ways throughout your life; each time that happens, you can use the questions and exercises I share to orient yourself and find a way forward.

My clients leave their first session with me inspired by their new understanding of how they are part of the problem, armed with the confidence of having a couple new experiments to try to get unstuck. They then arrive at the second session dispirited because they had thought that knowing the concept would be enough, and instead found they struggled to make a different choice despite their best intentions. Here's how that conversation goes:

Me: Did you try the experiment?

Them: Yes.

Me: That's great!

Them: But I only did it once! I thought I would be able to do it consistently now that I know what to do.

Me: But you did it once. One is greater than zero, which is how many times you would have done it otherwise. What results did you get?

Them: It went better than I expected.

Me: Great! Maybe you'll try the experiment again now that you've gotten some positive results. And as you practice the behavior over time, you'll translate your insight into a new habit.

This will not be an easy path. But I have applied these principles to transform my own life over the last decade, starting from my epiphany that I had a choice between burning myself out to meet the unrealistic expectations of my job or trying something different. Now, I decide how I spend my time each day, inspired by the work I do to help others make the kinds of transformational changes I made to my life and career while also committing the time and energy to be the father and partner I want to be.

In this book, I share what I have used to help people break through the assumptions and expectations that have kept them stuck, exhausted, burnt out, and miserable. It starts with one core concept:

You have a choice.

If you take this concept seriously and change your behavior as a result, you will find your own path forward. You will no longer feel stuck in a life that doesn't fit you, and instead intentionally create a meaningful life for yourself.

Let's begin.

CHAPTER 1

Aim

Alice: Would you tell me, please, which way I ought to go from here?

*The Cheshire Cat: That depends a good
deal on where you want to get to.*

Alice: I don't much care where.

The Cheshire Cat: Then it doesn't much matter which way you go.

—Lewis Carroll, *Alice in Wonderland*

*Ask yourself, "Why do I care about this? What is my mission?
What do my glory days look like?" Knowing what your
intentions are will help you bring about your goals; you
can't reach your goals if you don't know what they are.*

—Arlan Hamilton, *It's About Damn Time*

How do you want your life to be different?

It doesn't make sense to start moving until you have a clearer idea of where you want to go. When I ask people the above question, they generally answer with specific goals such as:

- I want to get promoted.
- I want a new job.
- I want a different manager.
- I want to be rich.
- I want to retire.

And then I ask them: **"What would be different about your life if you achieve that goal?"**

That's where things get more interesting and personal. Responses might include:

- I want to get promoted: people would listen to me more, and I would get to do more interesting work.
- I want a new job: I wouldn't be as stressed and miserable each day going to work.
- I want a different manager: I would feel valued as a person.
- I want to be rich and/or I want to retire: I would be able to do what I want each day without worrying about money. I wouldn't have to deal with a job that makes me miserable.

They've gone one level deeper in identifying the emotional needs such as love, safety, belonging, and autonomy that they hope to fulfill by achieving their goal. With that context, we can start to explore possibilities that address those emotional needs directly, rather than use an external proxy such as a new job or title or more money to satisfy that need.

Exercise 1.1

Now it is time for you to start on this journey of exploration and creation. Please reflect on the following questions and write down your answers:

1. How do you want your life to be different? Be specific—what would success look like in five years if you got what you wanted?

2. What would be different about your life if you achieved that goal? Imagine your life in that future—what would you be doing each day? How would you feel as you went about your day?

3. As you compare that future life to your current life, what's missing today? What emotional needs are not being met by your current life?

It is important to actually answer the questions, not just think about them. You could write them in a paper journal, type them into a document, or even dictate them into a notes app. But you must distill your answers from the inchoate thoughts swirling around in your head so you can review them later.

Part of why you might resist this exercise is that you don't want to confront the answers. My clients often physically recoil when they answer these questions, as they realize what they just said out loud. That recoil or physical discomfort is a sign that we are getting to the heart of the resistance that is keeping them stuck in their current life. I would love for you to keep asking yourself "How would that be different?" until you have such a reaction.

Imagine new possibilities

Building on the desire for autonomy identified in the last bullet point before the exercise, "I would be able to do what I want each day," another question I ask is, "What would that be? If you had all of your financial and physical needs satisfied, what would you do with your time and energy?"

The first answer is generally a variation of "lie on the beach and relax all day." That is understandable, as I frequently talk to people who feel burned out and exhausted. Some of them haven't taken a vacation in over a decade, so they may need months if not years of recharge time to remember who they are when they are not over-whelmed and stressed.[1]

But I persist and ask: "After you rest and recharge enough to want to do something other than lie around, what would you do?" What starts coming up at this point is beautiful and poignant as people reconnect to what matters to them.

I believe that most people want to make a difference in the world in some way. That could include being a good parent to their children, making art or music or food that others appreci-ate, being a good friend to others, helping their community, or investing in their own potential. As many people learned during the COVID-19 pandemic, just sitting around and watching TV or movies all day gets boring; most of us want to produce some-thing or contribute to something greater than ourselves, rather than just consume.

---

[1] For the first ten years of my career, I would work for two years, then change jobs. A friend asked me why I changed jobs every two years, and I gave the stan-dard reasons of feeling like I wasn't learning any more, I wanted new challenges, etc. He persisted and asked what else happened when I changed jobs. I said I generally took off three to four weeks between jobs. Then he asked, "Have you ever considered that maybe you just want a long break to recharge every two years?" My jaw dropped as I had not considered that possibility. I started doing that at Google, which is why I lasted over 10 years there.

So, what would a completely free version of yourself do if you had "f*** you money"? Suppose you could say no to any incoming task at work that was annoying,[2] and could choose to only do things that you found meaningful and impactful each day. What would that look like? Some possibilities might include:

- Returning to your initial motivation for choosing a career, the thrill of creation that you had in college that was beaten down under the pressure of constant delivery and production

- Choosing a path not taken, the art you might have chosen if you hadn't been pressured by parents or society to "do something responsible"

- Choosing to serve people or a community[3] and finding ways to make their lives better

These imagined possibilities offer a clue as to what activities might fill your emotional needs directly, rather than through the proxies filtered through the constraints of your present life, as described in the previous section of this chapter.

Until you give yourself time to slow down and reflect, you will not create the space to hear that quiet voice inside you that knows what you find meaningful. It may be no more than a faint echo that

---

[2] Greg McKeown (2014) starts off his book *Essentialism* with the story of a corporate executive who was so frustrated by his job that he was ready to quit because he was "majoring in minor activities" (1). He dreamed of coming back as a consultant so he could focus on the work that mattered and ignore all the busywork. A mentor told him to just start acting as if he already were that consultant, and to say no to meaningless work. The result: "Instead of making just a millimeter of progress in a million directions, he began to generate tremendous momentum towards accomplishing the things that were truly vital." (3)

[3] I was inspired by Jacqueline Novogratz's (2020) book, *Manifesto for a Moral Revolution*, in which she shares stories of entrepreneurs and innovators around the world who seek to make things better. She starts by asking them, "Who do you stand with?" (193). Once you choose a community to stand with, you can identify their problems and work to solve them.

has been drowned out by the much louder voices in your life and the media clamoring for your attention. But when you tune into that authentic inner voice, you will feel different. It can provide the direction to help guide your choices each day to bring yourself into greater alignment with your calling.

Exercise 1.2

Please reflect on the following questions and start to tune in to that inner voice:

1. What would you do with your time if you could do anything?

   - Please don't dismiss anything as unrealistic—pretend you just won the lottery and have no other commitments.

   - Write down at least 10 dream options in your journal, no matter how ridiculous they might seem.

2. For each dream option, take a moment to project yourself into that future. What do you feel as you imagine yourself doing that activity?

Your body will tell you the difference between options that are aligned with your inner voice, and options that are directed by external or cultural forces. With the externally directed options, you will feel pressure, tension, or resentment, which are a result of doing what you "should" or "must" do—it will feel like more of the same stuckness, like playing more Tetris.

Your authentic inner voice will feel different. You will feel a sense of calm excitement, of being energized and "in the flow," where you can get lost in doing the activity because it's an expression of your true self.[4] Those are the options that we will want to continue exploring throughout this book.

_____

[4] In Hinduism, the work that is yours to do is called your dharma, or sacred duty. I am grateful to Stephen Cope's book, *The Great Work of Your Life* (2012), for introducing me to the concept from the Bhagavad Gita and for sharing stories of what it takes to find and embrace your dharma. Reading his book convinced me to pursue coaching as my potential dharma.

This exercise might seem pointless if the options that arise do not provide for your financial well-being. But let's use our two principles to reframe that into a choice we can make about how we spend our time:

What isn't working for you?

I can't do the thing I want because I would not earn enough money to support my lifestyle.

How are you the problem?

I don't see the point of doing something if I don't get paid. I act as if the only reason to do something is to earn money.

You have a choice.

I can do an activity for love rather than for money. I can choose to spend time each week to create art for my own joy, volunteer to serve my community, or play around with technology for no other reason than because I want to.

Investing even a little time each week in what you find meaningful or enjoyable can have surprisingly positive effects on your life. You may re-awaken your own sense of agency and creativity and stop feeling like the only reason to do something is because you get paid or because you "have to." "Because I want to" is reason enough. That's one way to start filling your emotional needs directly without relying on proxies or external sources.

Seek energizing activities

You can also track your energy to orient yourself.

Imagine two people:

- Person A is great at the technical skills of their job but is drained by their work. They go home at the end of the day exhausted, wanting to do nothing more than to watch TV and survive until the weekend.

- Person B is great at the technical skills of their job, **and** they love the craft of their work. They are excited about the problems they work on each day, and they come home with energy to invest in their family and relationships, practice their craft, or work on the problems that engaged them at work that day.

I was once Person A. After I dropped out of graduate school, I became a software engineer because I was good at getting computers to do what I wanted. I was competent enough to keep writing code in my next few jobs.

Several years later, I worked at a start-up with Brett, who was the lead engineer. When we went out for beers on a Friday night, I asked him what he was up to that weekend. Brett told me excitedly that his fiancé had to work late that night, so he could go home and code for four more hours! With an unexpectedly free Friday night, the thing he most wanted to do was to keep coding.

That was why Brett was better than me as an engineer—and the gap was widening. I did not play with the latest programming languages in my free time, nor did I create open source or other projects to test out new techniques. I showed up each day to do my job and solve the problems in front of me, but then went home and did other activities. I was never going to be able to keep up with Brett in terms of my professional development because I just didn't love coding the way he did. The fact that he was energized by his work made him a better engineer.

What did I enjoy in the same way? It didn't occur to me at the time, but I could have looked at what I was doing on the weekends to figure out what energized me. I spent my free time reading about psychology, sociology, organizations, and leadership, and writing about those topics on my blog. Once I had that insight, I started moving my career in that direction; now I love my job as an executive coach because I spend my days thinking about and working with those topics.

Exercise 1.3

Let's help you align with your true self by using your energy to guide you on a micro scale:

1. Every day for a week, take a moment to reflect at the end of each day. Consider what activities energized you throughout the day, and what activities drained you. Record those in two columns in your journal.

2. After a week, look back at your journal to see what patterns you notice.

Maybe you'll find that certain people or situations energize or drain you. Or that you have more energy at certain times of the day. Maybe you are drained by meetings but love the times you get into the coding flow with your headphones on. Or maybe you're the opposite—you love the energy of interactive meetings and are drained by time alone.

Your energy is a guide to what aligns with your true self, as you will be drained by working against your natural tendencies and energized by work that fits who you are. Based on the patterns you observe, what changes can you make to increase your energizers and decrease your drains?

You may not like what you find in this exercise! You may realize that your previous choices have created a life in which you spend most of your time on activities you find draining.

Let's use our framework to transform your problem into a choice:

What isn't working for you?

I am exhausted and drained by my job and/or life because I spend my days doing what I "should" do or "have to" do.

How are you the problem?

I have made commitments to my job and to others and am choosing to continue to honor those commitments even though they are draining me. I am not willing to try other possibilities because "this is who I am" or "it's too risky to change."

You have a choice.

I can use my energy journal to discover what works for me. Rather than continuing to engage in activities that are draining, I can choose to spend more time on what creates energy for me, at the potential cost of sacrificing some aspects of my current life.

I once coached a client who had been doing technology consulting work for a decade but was starting to feel stale. She was in a rut where she was doing the same old work that no longer energized her, but she couldn't figure out a path to a different career. We did an exercise where we quickly went through a long list of values and she wrote down the ones that sparked some excitement. I asked her how those values might show up in a job, and she got more and more animated as she described the activities that would let her express those values each day. Her insight was that she didn't just love technology for its own sake—she also loved figuring out how technology could be applied to solve people's problems.

A couple weeks later, she was at a concert with a friend and shared her new insight about the work that excited her. Her friend's jaw dropped and he said, "My company desperately needs somebody to do exactly that!" She started working with that company as a consultant, which led to them hiring her full-time as their director of customer success, and she's been happily doing variations of that work for five years now. But it started with finding that clarity on what energized and excited her.

As you tune into what energizes you, you can experiment with shifting your day-to-day activities, including what you do at your job, to spend more time on energizing activities and less time on draining activities. That doesn't mean you should spend zero time on draining activities, as that's unrealistic, but shifting the balance will mean more energy available to invest in the rest of your life, including working towards your dream options from exercise 1.2.

Practical tip: Different people are energized by different things. There is somebody out there who is energized by what you find draining, and vice versa. If you work with them, you can both spend more time on what you find energizing and ultimately have greater impact together.

For instance, I am a strategic big-picture, blue-sky thinker who is energized by seeing the grand scope of things and debating where to go, but drained by the details of implementing processes to make things happen. I had greater impact in my career when I partnered with a coworker who loved details and process-building but who felt overwhelmed and lost without a clear direction. That partnership allowed both of us to focus on what energized us, making us both more effective. As a result, we achieved more as a team than we could have as individuals.

* * *

In this chapter, I have shared a few exercises you can try to get a better sense of how you might want your life to be different:

- Identify the core emotional needs not being met in your life.
- Imagine the new possibilities you might pursue if you didn't have other constraints.
- Seek energizing activities.

You may not yet know how to change your life to embrace these new possibilities. And that's okay!

Making a change in your life is like hiking up a mountain—you don't jump straight to the top. You choose a path, and you start walking. You take one step, and then another, and then another, and if you keep taking those steps toward the top of the mountain, you will eventually get there. Like reaching the mountaintop, changing your life starts by committing to keep taking steps in your intended direction.

Maybe you take a few steps in a possible direction and then decide you don't like that path. You can always return to your present state with a renewed appreciation that you are *choosing* that situation, rather than being stuck in it.

It's normal to not have a clear picture of your path forward at this point. If you already knew what you wanted to do, you would be doing it! This chapter was intended to help you come up with a few options that have a hint of possibility. Real change rarely starts with an epiphany where a bright light shines down from heaven to tell you exactly what to do with your life.

As you get more in tune with how you feel and what you want, you will start noticing a few slight inclinations that nudge you in a direction. By quieting down to listen for your inner voice, no matter how faint, you will form an idea of where to aim your initial efforts and take an initial step. With time and further exploration, you will gain greater clarity on the paths available to you, which will then accelerate your journey.

But setting a direction isn't enough, as there may be aspects of reality (and yourself) that are keeping you from moving in that direction. In the next three chapters, we will explore how to assess those constraints and provide strategies to address them.

CHAPTER 2

Accept Yourself

Until you make the unconscious conscious, it will direct your life and you will call it fate.

—Carl Jung

We humans often create the very constraints that keep us stuck. We are so accustomed to our situation that we feel helpless, treating those constraints as immovable realities that can never be changed. We act like a tiger raised in captivity that still paces in the same contained area even after being released from its cage.

The frustrating truth is that *we* are the zookeepers in this story, in an example of the "How are you the problem?" principle. We create our own cages to limit the options available to us, generally based on stories and patterns we learned in childhood, and then use our life experiences to justify why those cages are necessary. We feel like we have no choice, even though we are the ones maintaining the cages that keep us stuck.

In this chapter, we'll look at how those cages are constructed to learn how to release ourselves.

Change the rules

One way you can tell you're trapped in a cage of your own devising is to listen for internal voices stating absolute rules: I "must" do X, or I "have to" do Y, or I "could never" do Z. Such rules are rarely absolute if they aren't laws of physics, but they feel permanent because they are tied to the identities that you hold.

For example, "I can't take time off, I've got too much to do" or "I could never say no to my manager" can shift quickly when you need to take care of a family member. Your "family" identity takes precedence over your "worker" identity in that new reality, and you suddenly find a way to re-juggle those job responsibilities to focus on your family priorities. Within the "worker" identity, you didn't have a choice, but when you shifted to a different identity, you could re-prioritize the tasks of the "worker" identity appropriately.

We don't consciously create these rules for ourselves. When we find something that works for us, our brains learn to keep doing it unconsciously and automatically to save time and effort—considering all of your options every time would be slow and incredibly inefficient! For example, doing what your manager tells you may have brought you success early in your career, so you then take it on as a rule of your personal operating system and treat each manager's directive as an absolute imperative.

In the introduction, I shared my story of burning out at Google. It happened because I unconsciously had a rule that "I must do all of the work that my manager gives to me," which was unsustainable in that job. Once I burned out and was lying sick in bed, I realized the rule was incomplete. I reformulated it to "I must do all of the work that my manager gives to me, *unless I accept the consequences of not doing that work*." Then I chose to accept the consequences (losing my chance at promotion and receiving a lower performance rating) and stopped doing the work. The key mental shift for me was identifying the unconscious rule and then changing it from one that was absolute and unquestionable to one where I could include other considerations before making a choice.

Let's use our framework to transform these absolute rules into choices:

What isn't working for you?

I am stuck because of a rule I follow, e.g., I *can't* say no to my manager because being a good employee means doing what my manager says.

How are you the problem?

I am unthinkingly applying absolute rules in situations where they may not be relevant; in the example above, it is possible for me to say no to my manager, but I don't want to consider that possibility. Though the rule may have served me when I first learned it (and then learned to follow it unconsciously), the situation may have changed, e.g., I may have other options that I did not previously have. Or maybe that rule applies to an identity I no longer value, and I can stop applying it in this new context.

You have a choice

I can pause and consciously consider the trade-offs or identities that are implicitly contained in that rule. To use my Google example above, I modified my rule to be "I must do all of the work that my manager gives to me, *unless I accept the consequences of not doing that work.*" I chose the identity that prioritizes taking care of myself over the identity of the "good" (submissive) employee.

I may still choose the same action after explicitly considering all of the available options, but I will be more aware that it is a choice I am making with intentional trade-offs, rather than a rule I can never break.

Privilege check: Breaking cultural rules has more severe consequences for some people than others. For instance, "I must respect the authority of a police officer" is a rule I could potentially challenge, whereas a Black man might get shot and killed for not immediately complying. Similarly, "I must not use illegal drugs" is a rule that is enforced for people with black or brown skin, but rarely against those with white skin, as Michelle Alexander (2020) details in her book *The New Jim Crow*. This discrepancy also shows up in the workplace, e.g., women who break the cultural stereotype of being submissive and compliant experience greater consequences than a man would for the same actions. Those increased consequences may mean making different choices about which rules to follow, but my point is to make those choices consciously, rather than automatically and unquestioningly. You may have more options than you believe, especially in different contexts.

Loosen the constraints

Engineers are familiar with overconstrained problems, in which there is no solution possible that meets all the desired requirements. In such a situation, the engineer can decide which requirements to prioritize and which to loosen or remove entirely. Such changes may disappoint the stakeholder who wanted that requirement, but the engineer chooses to prioritize building something tangible over the impossible task of keeping everybody happy.[1]

The same applies to the cages we build for ourselves. We create so many rules for ourselves that there are no actions we can take that will satisfy all the rules. That's why we feel stuck—there is no way to do everything that we "should" do, especially when we consider all the various identities we hold.

Instead, we can do what engineers do with overconstrained problems: choose a requirement to loosen or remove. Maybe we can let go of the rule that we must make our manager happy. Maybe we can disappoint the coworker who wanted us to do something.

To take a specific example, let's use the rule "I can never ask for help."[2] Even though that's an absolute statement, there are a few potential scenarios where someone might let themselves break their rule and ask for help:

- If they're sick or injured
- If they have something more important to do
- If they don't know how to do something and need to learn
- If doing a task would cost them greatly for some reason

---

[1] A similar message is in the book *The Courage to Be Disliked* by Ichiro Kishimi and Fumitake Koga (2018).

[2] To give credit, I watched Jerry Weinberg lead a woman through this exercise at the Amplifying Your Effectiveness conference in 2009 and was impressed at how skillful he was at helping her loosen her rule step by step until she had so much more space to operate than she thought she had.

By considering scenarios where they might break the rule, they loosen the constraint, such that asking for help is no longer an unthinkable[3] option. Instead, they realize that asking for help is a choice they can make when it serves them, creating more possibilities for action.

Let's apply our framework to loosen the constraints around an example from the beginning of chapter 1, where somebody wanted to get rich or retire so they could do what they want:

What isn't working for you?

I can't do what I want each day because I have to spend my days working at a frustrating job.

How are you the problem?

I have chosen a lifestyle that requires a certain amount of income. To earn enough to keep that lifestyle, I spend most of my day on unsatisfying work.

You have a choice.

Each of those is a constraint I could change—I could find a way to live on less money, or I could find a more satisfying job.

1. The Financial Independence, Retire Early (FIRE) movement offers ways to minimize the everyday costs of life so that one doesn't have to work as much (or at all!). If that feels like too drastic of a minimalist lifestyle, I am effectively choosing to work a stressful job to pay for a more expensive life.

2. I could explore how to shape my job to be less stressful and more meaningful for me each day, using exercise 1.3 as a guide.

---

[3] I mean unthinkable *literally*. When we have absolute rules like this, we have never articulated to ourselves what will happen if we break the rule; we just have an unbearable yucky feeling about it. It's not based in logic, but in avoiding some overwhelming emotion that shuts down the logical part of our brain and drives us into immediate action.

Exercise 2.1

Let's uncover some of the rules holding us back from our desired future.

1. Go back to your list of dream options from exercise 1.2 that describe what you might do with your life if you had no constraints.

2. For each option, write down "I can't do this because…" and write down all of the reasons that come to mind.

3. Look at your list of reasons and see if there are common patterns across your options that you can formulate into absolute rules, as discussed earlier in this chapter: "I could never do X" or "I must do Y."

4. For each rule, think of ways you could modify or loosen that rule.

As an example, let's say one of your dream options was "I would live in a small town in Italy, eating great food and drinking great wine each day." Write down all of the reasons "I can't do this because…" Some reasons might be:

- I don't speak the language.
- I don't have the right to live and work in Italy.
- I could never live so far from my family.
- I have to do something more valuable than enjoy food and drink.

The first two reasons are practical objections that could be addressed if you made the effort. The latter two reasons are self-imposed rules, and you could explore ways to loosen them, perhaps by recognizing that you don't see your family that regularly anyway so living in Italy might not change how often you visit, or that you would have plenty of time each day between meals to explore different ways to add value.

Doing this exercise will help you to become more aware of your self-imposed rules so you can explore ways of loosening them. From there, you can start designing experiments to test the new options available to you. For example, I once met a family in the Italian town of Orvieto, who traveled there with their kids every summer to explore the possibility of eventually moving there.

With that freedom to choose when to redesign the rules or loosen the constraints when the situation changes, we can be more adaptable and can pick the rules that let us thrive in the current situation.[4]

Understand the original context

There's a reason we put these rules in place for ourselves. It might be tempting to say we should throw out these rules or behaviors entirely, but they served us at a certain point in our lives—and

---

[4] I like how James Carse (1986) describes this flexibility in his book *Finite and Infinite Games*. He defines finite games as ones that are, well, finite. They have a start, they have an end, they have a defined set of rules that the players obey. The goal in a finite game is to win the game according to the rules. This most obviously applies to sports, but also applies to late-stage capitalism.[*] College admissions is a finite game—there are a limited number of spots at the top universities, and students are trying to win one of those spots. Many companies operate as finite games—the top X% get promoted, the bottom Y% get fired. We choose to obey the rules in hopes of winning the game presented to us, and we let the game define our reality in a process Carse calls "veiling."

The purpose of what Carse describes as infinite games is to continue playing the game. There is no end, and there is no winning. We change the rules in order for the game to continue. Carse cites art, music, science, and poetry as examples of infinite games.

When we play by the rules we are given, we are playing the finite games imposed on us by our family and our culture. When we decide to change the rules to play our own game, we are playing the infinite game.

---

[*] In the finite game of capitalism, there are three rules, as described by Lynne Twist in her book *The Soul of Money* (2003, 48–55):
1. There's not enough.
2. More is better.
3. That's just the way it is.

Rule 3 is critical because it implies that you can't question the rules. Reading Twist's book helped me recognize that I didn't have to accept those rules. Once I realized the opposite of each rule applied to me ("I have enough," "I don't need more," and "It doesn't have to be this way"), I freed myself to walk away from my high-paying job at Google.

may still serve us at points in the future. I recommend investigating the reasons you might have originally created the rule, so that you understand the circumstances in which that rule might still make sense. By doing so, you can apply the rule as a conscious and intentional choice, rather than an automatic reaction that you do without thinking.

One of my clients, who I'll call Sam, was newly hired into a C-level position at a startup and was struggling with a demanding CEO. He knew he needed to challenge the CEO's thinking and explain what his team needed. And yet he couldn't bring himself to say what he needed to say.

I asked Sam how the CEO made him feel and what other situations in his life made him feel like that. He said he felt small, and in doing so, realized the CEO unconsciously reminded him of his father. Sam had learned as a young child to play the peacemaker to placate his father and always agree, so that his father wouldn't get angry. Taking on that role from a young age had conditioned Sam over the years not to challenge authority figures.

Once Sam made the connection, he realized that the rule he had in place to "never speak back to authority" did not apply in his work situation, because he was no longer the son, but a company leader. He tried an experiment to change his default behavior of deferring, and instead challenged the CEO on an important issue where he was confident in his position. The challenge was well-received, and he became more effective in his role as he grew more comfortable with direct communication. While Sam hasn't changed his interactions with his father, he learned he could change the interaction rules he followed at work.

Like Sam, we create most of these rules as children to handle overwhelming emotions such as shame, embarrassment, or feeling unloved. We never want to feel those emotions again, so we create defense mechanisms or rules that help us avoid those situations. Those rules helped us get our emotional needs met as children, so they worked great for their original intention and in their original context! But we get ourselves stuck when we unconsciously apply them as adults in other contexts.

Getting unstuck requires becoming conscious of the rule's original context and then making a conscious choice about when to apply the rule and when not to, as we will explore in the next exercise.

Exercise 2.2

Please reflect on the following questions and write down your answers.

1. Pick one of the rules you discovered in exercise 2.1.
2. Imagine breaking that rule. What emotions or physical sensations come up for you as you imagine doing the opposite of what you are supposed to do? These may include strong, unpleasant emotions such as shame or disgust, because your brain is afraid of what will happen if you don't follow the rule.
3. Stay with those unpleasant feelings and ask yourself, "What other situations in my life have made me feel this way?" and "What is my earliest memory of feeling this way?"
4. Remember that original situation and explore how it made sense for you as a child to adopt that rule in that context.
5. Return to the dream option that activated that rule and see if it still makes sense to apply that rule in that context.

Privilege check: If you experienced serious childhood trauma, please do not attempt this reflection about childhood experiences without the support of a trained therapist. Bringing up unprocessed trauma can be very damaging without somebody to help you safely reprocess it and return to normal functioning. People with less privilege often have a lifetime of unprocessed painful exclusionary moments to which they adapted in ways that may seem harmful but were the best they could manage under the circumstances. Interfering with those adaptive mechanisms without addressing the underlying trauma can be dangerous.

You can't do it all

Part of what makes these rules confusing is that we have different rules for different contexts where "I" have to do this, "I" must do that, or "I" can't ever do the other thing. It feels impossible to do everything that "I" want to do, because "I" want to do so many things, sometimes including two opposite things in the same situation.

We are trained in school to believe there is always a "right" answer, which we can find if we only work hard enough or are smart enough. Classes and problem sets are constrained to focus on a limited domain where there can be a single right answer.

In the real world, however, we may struggle with multiple domains that have multiple, conflicting "right" answers. For instance, let's take my situation as I write these words:

- The "right" answer for my coaching business is to work harder and take on more clients, as I have a rule that more is always better when it comes to work.

- The "right" answer for my family is to spend more time with my kids and my wife, rather than letting my attention be dominated by work.

- The "right" answer as an author is to spend more time writing, withdrawing from other activities like my coaching or my family so I can focus on this book.

- The "right" answer for my physical health is to spend more time exercising, sleeping, eating better, and resting so that my body can continue to support my other activities.

- The "right" answer for my mental health is to spend more time meditating and journaling, and giving myself more time to recharge rather than overscheduling myself.

- The "right" answer as a social being is to spend more time with friends who help me feel like I belong, so that I feel less lonely and stressed.[5]

- The "right" answer as a citizen is to spend more time getting out the vote, working on social causes, and contributing to my community.

And there's still more! I "should" also be keeping up with the news, reading more books, cooking more meals at home, and learning new skills.

The reality is I just can't do it all. Neither can you. There is far too much to do, and no possible way to do all those things I "should" do. And yet I keep getting tripped up because I know the "right" thing to do in each area and feel like I "should" be able to do it.

The constraint, of course, is time and attention. I can't do it all because there's only so many hours in the day. Each individual commitment feels attainable, but they far exceed my capacity in aggregate.

So why do I have so many different ideas of what I should be doing?

The answer: there is no single unified "me."

---

[5] Reading the books *Together*, by Dr. Vivek Murthy (2020), the current Surgeon General of the United States, and *Lost Connections* by Johann Hari (2018) illuminated for me that humans are social animals who fundamentally need to connect, and that I was not investing enough in those social connections. In chapter 8, you will learn how I responded to that realization.

CHAPTER 3

Accept Your Parts

We may not be responsible for the world that created our minds, but we can take responsibility for the mind with which we create our world.

—Dr. Gabor Maté, *In the Realm of Hungry Ghosts*

Instead of a singular self, our brains have created many "parts"[1] to handle different situations, and those parts take over when their context is activated. The conflicting impulses we feel then make more sense: one part of "me" wants to do this based on one context, another part of "me" wants to do that based on another context, and "I" feel conflicted because I have different parts pulling me in different directions. Each part has its own "right" answer about what to do, but they don't align!

Our parts are defined by the rules and constraints we discussed in the previous chapter. Because the parts are generally created when we are children, they have a very simplistic view of the world, which is why they use absolute rules framed as "must" and "never" without any awareness of how rules may shift based on context. But their intent is good—they want to help!

Since becoming a parent, I have started to think of these parts as toddlers with good intentions and clumsy execution. They are like my young son, who wants to help me in the kitchen but is also prone to making mistakes as he loses focus—as he did recently in cracking an egg perfectly but missing the bowl, so the raw egg slid off the countertop and splattered onto the floor.

Similarly, our parts intend to be helpful when they jump in to show that they know what to do in a situation. But they have a toddler's limited skill and context awareness, so they only see one small piece of the situation—like my son focusing so hard on cracking the egg that he forgot to keep it over the bowl.

This mental shift was transformative for me in realizing that the parts of my mind and their associated rules are trying hard to help; they are just unaware and unskilled. So instead of beating myself (or my parts) up for leading me astray, I can approach them

---

[1] This "parts" terminology is from the therapeutic Internal Family Systems framework, created by Richard C. Schwartz (IFS Institute, n.d.), which I learned about in Steve March's Aletheia coach training described at https://integralunfoldment.com/acp.

with compassion and love, much like I did with my son, working with him to clean up the dropped egg rather than yelling at him for being incompetent.

This is a particularly valuable shift because parts are generally created as defense mechanisms, with rules designed to help me avoid difficult emotions like fear and shame and grief. Some of the parts I've identified in myself are:

1. A part that feels compelled to please other people and make sure they are happy, because that part does not want to feel abandoned

2. A part that responds with great anger when others tell me what I must do, because that part does not want to feel a lack of autonomy

3. A part that shuts down and does mindless tasks when it feels overwhelmed because it can't keep everybody happy; instead, it looks for a specific task like washing dishes or playing a phone game so that it can deliver on those more limited expectations

Each of these parts has a good intention—to help me avoid feeling difficult emotions—yet their strategies often get in the way of me achieving my conscious intentions and can even conflict with each other. Trying to please everybody (part 1, above) can make me feel overwhelmed (part 3) and angry that I can't do what I want (part 2), so unless I'm mindful of that pattern, I can cycle through those parts and be constantly stuck and unhappy.

When I instead approach each part with compassion and understanding, I can acknowledge its good intention and its effort to keep me safe. These parts were created in a childhood attempt to earn love, and so when I offer that unconditional love to them (and myself!), they can relax and let go of their rigid reactions. Within that safety of loving myself and my parts, I'm not in a constant state of defensiveness and tension, trying to avoid the difficult emotions of life; instead, I can be with whatever arises as my whole self. Rather than being stuck in a cage constructed out of the rules of my parts, I can more freely choose what to do and accept the consequences, as illustrated below by applying our problem/choice framework:

What isn't working for you?

I can't decide what to do. I feel pulled in many directions: I want to do this, I want to do that, and I can't figure out how to do it all.

How are you the problem?

"I" am stuck because I have a community of parts. Each part has different motivations and contexts that can overlap or conflict. The internal conflict I am feeling is because each action I consider is being blocked by a different part's rule, and I am cycling through parts endlessly like a tiger stuck in a cage.

You have a choice.

When I unconsciously follow the absolute rules of those parts without being mindful of their original context, I am overconstrained and stuck, because there is no answer that all of my parts can accept.

To get unstuck, I can translate those rules from "I must do X" to "part of me feels I must do X." Rather than let my parts determine my actions from their limited contexts, I can investigate the rules that each part holds, understand the context in which the part developed, and how its rules serve me.

With that greater awareness of the conflicting contexts, I can identify the different parts of myself in play, consider their intentions and perspectives, mediate between them, and intentionally choose what to do from a sense of wholeness.

Easier said than done, of course. We'll talk more about practices that support this mindfulness throughout the rest of this chapter. But let's start by getting you more familiar with your parts.

Exercise 3.1

We will use the exercises from the previous chapter to guide you in identifying your parts:

1. Recall the list of rules you discovered in exercise 2.1, when you explored what was keeping you from enacting your "dream" options.

2. For each rule, go through exercise 2.2, when you imagined breaking the rule, identified the unpleasant feelings that arose, and recalled the childhood experiences that might have led to the construction of that rule.

3. You have now identified a part that was created in childhood to avoid the unpleasant feeling of shame, anger, or grief that arose as a child. Imagine this part as a toddler learning the rules of the world:

    a) "If I drop a ball, it falls to the ground." (Cause leads to effect.)

    b) "If I talk back, then I get yelled at by my father and feel abandoned." (Cause leads to effect, so the part learns to not talk back to avoid that feeling of abandonment.)

4. Most people have a few dozen parts, and you don't need to identify them all in this exercise. But I do recommend going through this exercise to identify a few parts and look for ways in which they might conflict, e.g., "If I talk back, I feel abandoned," vs. "If I don't speak up for myself, I feel powerless."

Catch the parts in action

Seeing the bars of our cage is only possible when we can see the parts and rules that we have been holding unconsciously for our whole lives. But how do we bring them to consciousness? In the remainder of this chapter, I will share practices that can help you catch when your parts are acting without your awareness, and experiments to bring them into greater alignment with each other and with your whole self.

Let's take the example of a director (I'll call her Lucy) who was given the feedback that she needed to be clearer and more direct in her communications. Her team was swirling and confused because they couldn't get a straight answer out of her, and her message seemed to change depending on who she talked to. This was partly because she had several cross-functional stakeholders, each of whom wanted different things urgently, so she felt like she had to change the top priority for herself and her team after every meeting.

Lucy also wasn't holding low performers on the team accountable because she felt her job was to make everybody on the team successful even if they weren't doing their job. Instead of setting clear performance standards and letting people fail to deliver, she was doing people's jobs for them because she felt their failure was her failure. This tolerance was affecting the morale and performance of her team because they also had to cover for the low performers, and it was draining Lucy because she was doing their jobs as well as her own.

Yet she found herself using a "likable cheerleader" voice of encouragement with everybody and avoiding the direct conversations she needed to have with her stakeholders and her team. Her actions did not align with her conscious intent to be clearer and more direct, which was a sign that unconscious parts were at work.

I asked her, "How do you feel in that moment before speaking up?"

Anxiety and terror were what came up for her. She felt as if she were under so much tension that her life was under threat. When we explored a little more of her history, she revealed, "I used to be that direct and was called a bitch and difficult to work with." In fact, she had been fired from multiple jobs for not being "respectful" enough.

Her parts naturally wanted to protect her from those threatening conditions, so they took over and did what they had learned would create safety: do whatever it takes to please everyone around you, encouraging them and not holding them accountable. And that strategy worked! It made Lucy successful as an individual contributor creating fantastic work, and it got her promoted.

But "what got you here won't get you there,"[2] and those same people-pleasing tendencies were now keeping her from being successful as a director. She had too many people depending on her, and they all wanted different things; trying to keep them all happy was impossible, putting her into a constant state of anxiety and terror. No matter what she tried, somebody was unhappy, and her unconscious parts "knew" that if somebody was unhappy, she was going to be punished.

Her unconscious parts were now the problem, not the solution, as they were steering her away from the very actions she needed to take to improve her situation:

- Rather than have a direct conversation to hold people on her team accountable for their underperformance, she was enabling them and even doing their work for them, which meant she was falling behind on her own responsibilities.

- Rather than have a clear conversation about expectations with her VP and cross-functional stakeholders, she was saying yes to everything being asked of her, which created unreasonable amounts of work for her and her team, leading to burn out.

---

[2] To use Marshall Goldsmith's (2007) memorable book title.

That left her with a dilemma. Her unconscious parts were taking over and reacting before she even had a chance to think about how she intended to respond. She felt stuck because she could see how her previous patterns were no longer serving her, but she didn't see how to change those reactions.

Intention, attention, action

We all know of the New Year's resolution model for behavior change, which involves setting an intention to eat healthier or exercise more. This model rarely works to change our actions because we are not aware of how our current unconscious behaviors are serving us in some way (remember, those parts were created for a reason!).[3]

I prefer the model of Intention, Attention, Action: to achieve our Intention of taking different Actions, we must first focus our Attention on how and when our parts take over to follow a previously learned rule. Only by developing that awareness will we have a choice: to react as we always have, or to consciously choose a different Action that creates new possibilities.

Since Lucy now knew how she wanted to behave differently (she had set a clear intention), I asked her to pay attention to what was keeping her from that intended action by using a daily journaling exercise to answer the following questions:

- When today did I speak my mind directly and hold people accountable? What circumstances enabled that?

---

[3] Kegan and Lahey's (2009) Immunity to Change methodology is another structured way to find our unconscious rules. One amazing statistic from the Immunity to Change training came from a study of patients who had survived heart attacks and were told they had to change their diet and exercise patterns, or they might die from their next heart attack. Even under threat of death, only one in seven changed their behavior! That's how powerful our unconscious parts are, as they have a different agenda of love or safety or belonging that must be addressed directly before our conscious brains can choose different actions.

- When today did I hold my tongue and use my "likable cheerleader" voice instead? What circumstances contributed to that? How did I feel in those moments?

- What will I do differently tomorrow after reflecting on the questions above?

These questions were designed to bring her unconscious parts' reactions into consciousness, so she could start to notice them taking over and choose different actions instead.

Exercise 3.2

If you have set a conscious intention to change your behavior and actions, and are not following through on that intention, it's time to pay attention. Please reflect on the following questions daily and write down your answers to discover patterns of how your parts are unconsciously taking over and steering you away from an intended behavior change.

1. When today did I carry out my intended behavior? What circumstances enabled that?

    a) Enabling circumstances might include physical (different environments), personal (how well did you sleep or eat?) or social (different people) components.

2. When today did I fall back into my previous reactive behavior? What circumstances contributed to that? What did I physically feel like in those moments?

    a) Unconsciously defaulting to previous behavior is often the sign of a part taking over. Parts can be embodied as physical tension, e.g., a sinking feeling in the stomach, your heart racing, your breathing getting shallow and quick, a clenched jaw, a dry throat, or tight shoulders.

3. What will I do differently tomorrow after reflecting on the questions above?

    a) What can I do to create the circumstances that enable my intended behavior?

    b) How can I use the physical feeling of my parts taking over as a signal to reset and try something different?

This reflection will help you learn to catch those moments where your parts take over and interfere with your intention. If you practice this reflection daily and pay more attention to the tensions and feelings that arise when your parts take over, you will notice those moments more and more quickly until you can eventually catch them in real time. Once you develop this self-awareness, you can pause in the moment before reacting, decide which parts you will listen to, which parts' rules you will release or loosen, and then consciously choose a different action from your whole self.

Fight or flight

Why are these unconscious parts so powerful and limiting at the same time? The answer requires taking a small detour into the nervous system.

When you are under threat, your body switches into fight-or-flight mode, also known as the sympathetic nervous system. This floods the body with cortisol and adrenaline so that you can respond quickly to danger by fighting or escaping.

Another effect of these chemicals is that they narrow your attention—you become highly attuned to what is directly in front of you and lose your awareness of the larger environment. This makes sense from an evolutionary perspective: if a tiger is attacking you, you want to put your full attention on the tiger and nothing else until you are safe! In this mode, you are on high alert for danger, treating everything as a threat by default.

However, this narrow focus is an impediment in the complex contexts most of us find ourselves in each day, in which there are many "right" answers and no simple responses that satisfy all of our parts. With fight-or-flight "blinders" on, you are literally not aware of the greater complexity, so you default to the simple, programmed reactions of your parts.

But when each part perceives a threat to its pattern as a survival threat, your sympathetic nervous system is getting activated many times a day. While that makes evolutionary sense (it's better to overreact to potential danger than to be complacent and get eaten), it has several negative consequences:

- You are regularly being flooded with cortisol (the stress hormone) and putting long-term wear and tear on your body, which can lead to heart attacks, mental health issues, and other problems.

- You can't see other possibilities available to you due to the narrowed focus, and therefore are stuck without options.

- You treat everything as potential threats rather than seeing the possibilities of collaboration or cooperation that might be available to you.

For your long-term health and sanity, you need to learn how to distinguish actual life-threatening situations from the activation of your unconscious parts.

The first step is recognizing the signals that your body has activated fight-or-flight mode. Exercise 3.2 above can help you pay attention to what happens when your parts take over and to identify the associated intense feelings or physical sensations, such as your heart racing, your muscles tensing, or your breathing becoming fast and short. Your body is literally gearing up to fight or flee, so you will likely feel heightened energy from the adrenaline flooding your system.

Research shows that there are two other survival strategies for the sympathetic nervous system beyond fight or flight, which are freeze and fawn.[4] These additional survival strategies explain a lot of behavior that doesn't fit neatly into the fight-or-flight categories. Some people shut down and freeze, much like animals that play dead to avoid getting attacked by predators. In Lucy's case above, her parts' survival strategy was fawning: trying to please everybody around her to keep herself safe.

Once you identify your parts' go-to survival strategies and how they feel in your body, you can then look for those signals as an alert that the parts have activated your body into fight-or-flight mode—and you can choose to interrupt the process.

---

[4] I learned of these in Pete Walker's (2018) book *Complex PTSD: From Surviving to Thriving*.

Take a deep breath

We have all heard the advice to pause and take a deep breath before making a decision, but until a few years ago, I didn't know the science of why this works. Taking deep breaths is the signal to our nervous system to deactivate the fight-or-flight sympathetic nervous system and return to the calm, "rest and digest" parasympathetic nervous system. If you are actually facing a tiger, you will be taking fast, shallow breaths to get oxygen into your system so you can respond quickly. If you are taking calm, slow, deep breaths, you are clearly not in immediate danger and your body can relax into a more open and connected state.

Exercise 3.3

In exercise 3.2, you discovered the intense physical feelings that accompany the moments when your parts take over. These are signals that your body has been activated into fight-or-flight mode.

When you notice those signals and physical reactions, try these actions to interrupt the programmed response of your parts:

1. Pause and take a few deep breaths to start resetting your nervous system.[5] I recommend the box breathing technique:[6] you breathe in for four counts, hold for four counts, breathe out for four counts, and hold for four counts.

2. Remind yourself that you have a physical body by feeling your feet touching the floor or listening for your own heartbeat. This reconnection to your body reminds you that you are not in actual physical danger.

---

[5] You may have to experiment with different ways to ground yourself and reset your nervous system. Deep breaths work for me, but some people find that focusing on their breath triggers the fight-or-flight response. Other possibilities for regrounding yourself might include:

- Doing a body scan by bringing your attention to each part of the body as a way of getting out of your head.
- Tuning into your five senses: paying attention to what you can see, hear, touch, smell, or taste.
- Going for a walk and feeling the impact of each step on the ground.
- Going into nature and letting yourself soak in the expansive sensory experience. One version of this is forest bathing.

[6] The Cleveland Clinic (2021) describes the benefits of box breathing at https://health.clevelandclinic.org/box-breathing-benefits/

3. Depending on your particular fight-or-flight response, you can try different actions to release the tension and energy built up by the adrenaline and cortisol hormones.

   a) Fight: Do aggressive actions such as shadow box, jump up and down, or shout into a pillow.

   b) Flight: Go for a walk or run, or shake out your arms and legs to let your body act out its flight behavior.

   c) Freeze: Physically move or stretch to break the body's instinct to freeze. A habit of avoidance (e.g., a part of me escapes into playing games on my phone when I don't know what to do) can also be a form of freezing, so you can use your avoidance strategy as a signal to take a deep breath and start moving.

   d) Fawn: Take a few minutes to journal on what you wish you could say, so that you become more aware of the gap between what you think and your people-pleasing tendencies. Declaring that reality for yourself can help break that part's habit of apologizing and placating.

In my case, fight-or-flight mode tends to show up as me getting into a defensive posture with my shoulders tensed and curved in, as if to protect myself from a punch. So, when I notice myself in that mode, I pause, remind myself I am safe, take a few deep breaths, and open up my chest and consciously relax my shoulders. The mind follows the body, and once I relax my body, my mind lowers the "blinders" and lets me see more options. You will have to experiment to discover what works for you.

According to the research of Harvard neuroanatomist Dr. Jill Bolte Taylor,[7] the hormones activated by fight-or-flight mode will clear out of your system in just 90 seconds once the threat has passed. This may seem impossible if you have had the experience of being stuck in an angry or resentful state for hours if not days. She suggests that when you have that experience, you are retriggering the emotion repeatedly by thinking of the conditions that you and your parts consider threatening.

Dr. Robert Sapolsky's (2004) book *Why Zebras Don't Get Ulcers* similarly describes how, after animals in the wild go into fight-or-flight mode, they release their bodily tension and quickly return to their resting state once the threat has passed. But in our world of chronic stress, we stay in fight-or-flight mode. Our systems aren't designed to operate with those elevated levels of stress hormones, and thus experience cumulative damage unless the stress is released.

When my kids were babies, they would sometimes get angry about not getting what they wanted and would scream at the top of their lungs. Surprisingly, after they expressed the emotion, they would regularly become calm again within a minute. Their behavior gives a clue as to why mindfulness practices are so effective at lowering stress. If we feel our feelings and express them, they can

---

[7] Dr. Bolte-Taylor's research is described in the *Psychology Today* article "The 90-Second Rule That Builds Self-Control" (Robinson 2020).

be processed by our body and we can move on. But most of us in Western cultures are taught that men can't show any emotion but anger, and women can show any emotion except anger, so we hold those "unacceptable" emotions tightly inside, unprocessed, leading to great tension.[8]

So, when you notice your parts taking over by recognizing the physical signals identified in exercise 3.2, take a moment to breathe deeply and feel what you are feeling.[9] As I tell my son, that doesn't mean that you act from the feeling—just because he is feeling angry, he doesn't get to hit his sister. But naming the feeling helps to identify what's going on with our body, so we can interrupt unconscious reactions and instead be more consciously aware; for example, "I am feeling angry, and I want to yell at somebody. Instead, I will take a deep breath and find a more productive response."

I have also found that merely naming the feeling is often all that a part needs to relax. Like a toddler who seeks attention from their parents, turning to a part and saying, "I see you and the big feelings that you have!" can be enough to release the part's tension. All humans want to feel seen and acknowledged, and our parts have that same need.

---

[8] I have personally experienced how EMDR (Eye Movement Desensitization and Reprocessing) therapy can be powerful in releasing emotions that were bottled up inside me for decades by finally emotionally processing a situation where I felt shame at the time and never acknowledged it. Peter Levine's (2016) somatic experiencing approach in his book *Waking the Tiger* describes something similar, although I don't have personal experience with that method.

[9] This can sometimes be difficult to do, as we often have multiple parts and feelings operating at once. For instance, a situation may trigger a part to feel shame. To defend us from feeling hurt in that way, a "firefighter" part may get triggered to flood the body with anger and the "fight" reflex. One aspect of emotional intelligence is learning to deconstruct that emotional cocktail into the components of shame (the feeling) and anger (the feeling about the feeling).

Love your parts

Emotions can feel overwhelming to the point where we identify with them, e.g., "*I am* angry." Our parts can similarly overwhelm us such that we identify with them and can't see any other possibilities.

What I've learned[10] is that this is not a coincidence: strong emotions come from our parts. Our parts feel that things "should" be[11] a certain way and when things don't turn out that way, they get angry, sad, or scared. The good news is that our whole, integrated self is resilient and can accept whatever happens, and we can reconnect to that self when we recognize what's happening and disidentify with our parts.

I love Ann Weiser Cornell's simple exercise to create that separation from our feelings and parts. Using the example of anger, here's how the sequence of transformation works:

1. *I am* angry.

2. I am *feeling* angry.

3. *Part of me* is feeling so angry right now.

With this disidentification, we can now treat our parts as separate entities to whom we can offer compassion and support when they are struggling with big emotions.

What can make our parts feel overwhelming is that they are often internalized versions of authority figures from early in our lives, who feel much bigger than us. If a big internal voice says, "You must do X," then you shut up and do X. That immediate,

---

[10] Thanks to Ann Weiser Cornell's teachings on focusing at https://focusingresources.com/, and Steve March's extension of focusing with his Aletheia coaching methodology described at https://integralunfoldment.com/acp.

[11] Tracy Goss (2010) describes this as the "Universal Human Paradigm" in her book *The Last Word on Power*, "There is a way things should be. And when they are that way, they are right. When they're not that way, something is wrong with you, them or it."

unthinking obedience is how our parts get us into difficult situations with no easy answers.

As I mentioned earlier in this chapter, I find it helpful to think of parts as toddlers who have good intentions but sometimes get overwhelmed by situations. They are not powerful voices that know better than me; they are little kids doing the best they can to navigate a complex world. When they get louder, they are throwing a tantrum about being ignored, so it helps to acknowledge them and the big feelings they are feeling. As the parent of a toddler, I've learned that the best response to a tantrum is for me to calmly respond with love and connection because they are emotionally out of control and need me to calm them down rather than getting emotionally activated myself. Similarly, when our parts are overwhelmed, they need an acknowledgment of their situation and warm compassion and support, similar to what we would offer to a friend or loved one going through a tough time.

To do so, you can imagine having a conversation with your parts. The script could go something like this (and it can help to speak this out loud):

"I see you, little part, feeling so angry right now because you didn't get what you wanted. You have been working so hard and doing everything you can to get that result, and it didn't happen. That's so frustrating! Let me give you a big warm hug to let you know how much I appreciate your efforts to keep me safe—you are working so hard, and I see that. Thank you! But please take a step back so we can try something different this time, and I promise it is safe for us."[12]

You might call this re-parenting your parts, giving them the loving parenting and appreciation they didn't receive in childhood, which is why they had to come up with other strategies to earn love,

---

[12] I recently discovered that this is essentially what Dr. John Gottman (1998) calls "Emotion Coaching" in his book *Raising an Emotionally Intelligent Child*.

safety, and belonging.[13] By seeing them, and acknowledging and honoring their perspective, you are directly satisfying their emotional needs and giving them the love they desire, so they don't feel as compelled to enact their previous strategies to fill those needs.

Calming your parts gives you the space to make a choice about what you will do next:

- You can follow your previous pattern and let your parts unconsciously choose actions that follow the survival rules they developed to get their needs met; or

- you can act as the wise, calm parent of the family of your parts, listen to their input, and then choose a more intentional path through the world.

This brings us back to the story of my client Lucy from earlier in this chapter. Lucy grew more aware through these practices of how her parts were taking over and feeling anxiety and terror whenever somebody was unhappy. By taking a deep breath and acknowledging that her parts were feeling such terror, she was able to separate herself from her parts and let go of the humiliation and shame they felt when things weren't working out as they "should." As Lucy released the constraints her parts had imposed on her, she felt a great sense of freedom, of "I can do what I want to do," allowing her to map a new path chosen from her whole self.

---

[13] These are the core human emotional needs according to Jerry Colonna in his Reboot podcast at https://www.reboot.io/podcast/. He regularly helps the people he coaches on the podcast see how their unwanted behaviors relate to a childhood pattern they learned to ensure love, safety, or belonging.

CHAPTER 4

Accept Others

When someone shows you who they are,
believe them the first time.

—Maya Angelou

In chapter 3, you learned how "you" (aka your parts) create your own cages and keep yourself constrained with rules that previously helped you earn love, safety, and belonging and/or protected you from feeling "negative" emotions. You developed awareness of the signals that indicate when those parts are taking over in exercise 3.2, so you can address their emotional needs directly rather than unconsciously enact their rules. With this approach, you can consciously choose actions that align with your intentions, rather than being derailed by your parts.

You might be thinking, "But that still doesn't solve my stuckness! Even if I get out of my own way, I still have to deal with all of these other people who are being unreasonable—my boss, my coworkers, my spouse, my parents, my kids. They are the ones keeping me stuck, not me!"

In this chapter, we will investigate how true that claim is, and what we can do in those interactions to get different results.

Accept others as they are

In Buddhist philosophy,[1] our suffering is a consequence of the gap between our expectations and reality. When we drop a ball, we expect it to fall to the ground, so when it does, we don't feel frustrated because it happens every time. In other situations, we create our suffering and discontent by yearning for a different outcome.

We have many unconscious expectations of what other people "should" do, based on our previous life experiences, or perhaps from consuming media that shows us how people "should" behave. When another person does not do what they "should," we get frustrated and blame them for not conforming to our expectations.

---

[1] I have not studied Buddhism in depth, but this is my interpretation based on a few explanations I've read.

The root cause of our suffering in that interaction is not the other person, but our model of what they "should" do. For instance, you might hold the following beliefs:

- My coworker "should" want to work with me and do what I ask of them.
- My manager "should" look out for me and support me in difficult situations.
- My company "should" make sure I'm appropriately compensated and promote me without me asking. I "shouldn't" have to play politics to get what I deserve.
- My spouse "should" take care of me and never hurt my feelings.

If your coworker, manager, company, or spouse doesn't live up to those ideals, you will be frustrated with them, even though they never made those commitments and regularly behave differently.

Let's take an example of a client, who I'll call Emma. Emma was frustrated with her manager, leading to the following discussion.

Emma: I want my boss to have my back and protect me by handling this difficult situation.

Me: What evidence do you have that your manager would act that way?

Emma paused and realized she had rarely seen her manager protect and support her in the way she wanted. Her manager's actions had mostly served to protect her own reputation.

Me: If you have seen how she responds, why are you surprised or frustrated by her behavior?

Emma: Shouldn't a manager protect their team, and work to help them grow? I try to do that as a manager. Why doesn't my manager do that?

Me: I don't know why your manager doesn't do that. But you have repeatedly told me that she doesn't. If you accept that she will not change, nor support you in that way, what would you do differently?

That question shook her, and it led to the transformation outlined below:

What isn't working for you?

Emma had been framing the problem as her manager not doing what she "should" be doing, so Emma was looking for ways to "make" her manager step up and act the way she wanted her to act. But we can't control the behavior of others. We only control our own actions.

How are you the problem?

Emma had been waiting for her manager to change and was putting all of the responsibility to change the situation on her manager. Emma tried to model the behavior she wanted from her manager, but otherwise abandoned her own ability to do anything other than hope her manager would "wake up." This left Emma stuck when her manager didn't change.

You have a choice.

After I asked her what she would do differently, Emma realized she could stop hoping her manager would provide the support she desired and gave herself the agency to change the situation to get what she wanted.

- Rather than wait for her manager to handle difficult situations, Emma took action to handle them herself.

- Rather than yearn for positive feedback from her manager, Emma paid more attention to the feedback from her peers and team and started giving herself credit for how she was keeping her team happy and productive in a chaotic environment.

- Rather than hope her manager would ensure her promotion, Emma started meeting with her key stakeholders to secure their support.[2]

It's not others, it's our parts

An analogy I use with my clients in these situations is playing video games. If you are playing a game where you have to beat a big "boss" character to clear a level, you don't say "the boss should do X" and then get frustrated that the boss doesn't do X. You observe what the boss does, and come up with a strategy to defeat them with the tools you have available.

You might find it difficult to be that analytical when dealing with real people because you get frustrated or otherwise swept away emotionally. Those strong emotions are a signal that your parts are surfacing. As we discussed in the previous chapter, our parts activate emotions because they have a simplistic view of the way the

---

[2] This was a risky choice because Emma could have faced consequences. Her manager could have treated her actions as a threat and punished her in retribution, either formally through performance feedback in an evaluation or by diminishing her work through informal channels. This had happened in the past, so Emma's fear of retribution had been keeping her stuck and feeling like she had to accept the abusive behavior of her manager.

However, her manager's behavior became so intolerable that Emma was ready to quit for the sake of her mental health. That's when meeting with key stakeholders became a more viable choice. If her manager had gotten her fired in response, it would have been a better outcome for Emma than quitting, because at least she would get a severance package. I encouraged her to try the option she feared, and she discovered that her peers and other stakeholders supported her more than she imagined possible.

world "should" be, much like a toddler. And like a toddler, our parts get frustrated and angry when the world does not conform to their desires.

When you can calm your parts down and adjust your expectations of others to match their actual behavior, you will no longer be surprised or frustrated by what they do and can then choose actions that take that reality into account—much like playing a video game.

This requires letting go of the expectations that your parts have, which means applying what we learned in the previous chapter: notice when your parts are taking over, and then pause to reset your nervous system to get out of survival mode, as we practiced in exercise 3.3. From that calmer, wider perspective, you can observe what is happening without the blinders of expectations, and let go of what your parts think "should" be happening.

This is why many spiritual traditions practice mindfulness, the skill of being present with whatever is happening rather than interpreting events around us through the cage of our "shoulds." I once read about an extreme version of presence where Zen Buddhist monks in training go out three times a day in the winter to dump buckets of ice water over themselves (Cain 2019a). The anticipation and expectations that they (or I would say their parts) held around the experience could make it horrific. But when they meditated and could be completely present to the experience without expectations, it was merely unpleasant (I offer exercise 4.4 at the end of this chapter as a much milder version of this practice). The suffering came from the expectations, not the ice water.

The same applies to our interactions with others. The suffering and the stuckness do not come from others, but from the expectations of our parts. *We* are the problem.

A personal example is how I interacted with my mother as an adult. My mom grew up in Korea and was the typical "tiger mom," pushing me to succeed in classes and extracurricular activities that would get me into college (e.g., she started me on violin lessons at age three). As an adult, I resented her focus on my achievements and on my lack of a wife and children, as I (and my parts) wished she would instead unconditionally support me as I was. In retrospect, I realize her own parts were pressuring her about what my life "should" look like if she had been a good mother.

When I started therapy in my forties, my therapist had essentially the same conversation with me that I had with my client above:

Therapist: What evidence do you have that she will behave differently? Has she shown any signs in the 40+ years you have known her?

Me (sheepishly): No.

Therapist: Okay, so rather than resent her and hope that she will change, what will *you* do differently?

My parts wanted a mom that would support and love me unconditionally and kept hoping that she would change. But that's not who she was. As a result, every interaction with my mom left me (and my parts) angry and resentful that she wasn't the mom I (they) wanted.[3]

Over a couple years, I reset my expectations about my mother to accept that her priority was telling stories about my achievements to her friends to illustrate what a wonderful mom she was. With that understanding, my interactions with my mom became much less tense and angry because I learned to accept who she had always been and give her the stories she wanted. She still triggered

---

[3] I was once complaining to a good friend about how I was always furious after interactions with my mother, and I didn't understand how she could get me so angry when other people couldn't. His response: "Of course your mother knows where your buttons are—she installed them!"

my parts occasionally, but I learned to pause, take a deep breath, and respond with tactics that worked to defuse the situation.[4]

More generally, we can transform our issues with others into a choice we make, as follows:

What isn't working for you?

The other person is the problem. They are not behaving the way they should, and I am justifiably angry that they aren't seeing reason or changing in the way I want.

How are you the problem?

I am stuck in the perspective of my parts, who have rigid ideas of how others "should" behave or "must" behave. I am judging the other person by these expectations even though they have never committed to those rules. My anger and frustration come from the difference between my expectations and the behavior of the other person, even though they behave consistently by their rules.

You have a choice.

Rather than staying angry while waiting in vain for the other person to change, I can update my expectations about them to match their actual behavior. With that clarity, I can choose different ways to handle our interactions.

---

[4] I became particularly fond of what my therapist called the "broken record" technique of deciding on a message and unemotionally repeating it over and over and over again. Instead of getting frustrated and arguing with my mother, I would say, "Yes, I know you think I should be dating more, but now is not a good time for me" and "I hear that you want me to get married, but for now I'm focusing on other things," etc., until she got bored and moved on to a different topic.

Exercise 4.1

This last choice—to update your expectations—is difficult! It's much easier to blame the other person for not changing than to take responsibility for changing yourself. But as we discussed in the introduction chapter, you can't change others, so let's lay out the steps you can take in a situation where you are frustrated with somebody else who is not behaving as they "should."

1. Recognize when you are being taken over by a part who wants the other person to behave differently. The strong emotions you feel amid a whirlwind of thoughts are that part throwing a tantrum because it isn't getting what it wants, much like a toddler not getting an ice cream cone. Look for the physical signals of your parts taking over that you discovered in exercise 3.2.

2. Get yourself out of that fight-or-flight activated state. We explored some ways to do that in exercise 3.3, but a good place to start is taking several deep breaths and perhaps asking the part to step back even though it is trying to help you with the "unfair" situation.

3. Once you are calmer and don't have the emotions and adrenaline coursing through you, observe the other person and objectively describe their behavior, in the way a scientist might with an animal subject. Write down what they do in your interactions without letting your parts interject "But they should do X!" or "Why aren't they doing Y?"

4. While still in your calm state, ask yourself, "If this person does not change their behavior, what can I do to handle them differently so that I get more of what I want from the interaction?" Pretend you are advising somebody else in your situation, as it's much easier to see what to do when you're not involved and getting your parts triggered.[5] Once you identify a few new actions to try, start experimenting with those possibilities to see what helps your situation. If nothing else, you can start minimizing your interactions with that person rather than expect them to be helpful.

---

[5] I can't tell you how many times my therapist or coach has given me advice, and I say "I just told two clients that same advice this week! How could I not have seen that it applies to my situation as well?"

Note that acceptance is not the same as approval, as we will discuss later in this chapter. You may still feel that the other person should behave differently, and that you don't approve of their behavior. But you will be more effective if you accept that their current behavior patterns are unlikely to change, and plan for that reality.

It's not others, it's their parts

When we observe how others behave, without being taken over by our parts that are expecting something different, we may realize that they are acting out *their* parts. Their parts have their own expectations of others, and simplistic beliefs of how the world "should" be and how others "should" treat them. Just like our parts, their parts get frustrated and angry when the world does not conform to their desires, and they act out that frustration like the toddlers who adopted these simplistic views to adapt to their childhood environment.

So, when you see somebody else losing their temper after being triggered by something you said or did, **it's not about you**. One of their parts is throwing a tantrum because the world is not acting as it "should," in that you are not conforming to what it wants or its rules.

Unfortunately, what often happens is that the anger of the other person's part triggers one of our parts to feel shame, so we act out our own response to the shame, where we either get furious ourselves (fight), get defensive (flight), shut down (freeze), or placate (fawn). Now we have an interaction between two parts, which, if you've seen two toddlers fight over a toy, does not end well.

The tactics described in the previous chapter can help. Pause. Take a few deep breaths to interrupt the fight/flight/freeze/fawn reflex, and reset your nervous system, as described in exercise 3.3.

Recognize that the other person is acting from a part, and focus on what you can control, which is your response.

You wouldn't expect a rational discussion to convince a screaming toddler in the middle of a tantrum, so don't try to argue with this person when they are taken over by their part. Instead, mirror and reflect their desires to calm them down by repeating what they're saying in their own words, because parts want to be heard and validated; for example, "I hear how upset you are that this wasn't done the way you wanted." This can help to de-escalate the situation, allowing you both to emerge from the fight-or-flight state and hopefully return to have a calmer and more productive discussion later.

A variation on this scenario is when somebody accuses you of something awful. Most of the time, it's not about anything you've done, but a projection of their deepest, darkest fears onto you. They assume that everybody else is like them and that you are doing what one of their parts wishes they could do. Once you learn this mental shift, you can stop feeling attacked by their accusations and instead use those moments to develop insight into the other person. If they say, "Nobody likes working with you," they just told you their own fear. People that accuse others of infidelity are the ones most likely to be considering it themselves—since they spend their time thinking about it, they assume others are as well. Again, it's not about you!

To use the example from earlier in this chapter, I suspected that Emma's manager was being taken over by a part that was trying to keep her safe. That part focused on "How will this affect me?" because it felt deeply unsafe at some point in her life, and therefore did not trust others to collaborate or look out for her. Her part didn't see any benefit in helping people, and therefore projected her own self-centeredness onto others because of those formative experiences.

Once I helped Emma see that this lack of caring was not specific to her and was more about her manager's parts acting up, it helped Emma take her manager's behavior less personally and find a new path forward. In particular, since we hypothesized that her manager's part felt threatened by Emma's competence, Emma started giving her manager more positive feedback, which helped her manager relax. This technique of offering more safety and belonging to her manager's part was effective in getting Emma more freedom and space to advance her agenda.

This may seem like catering to the manager's dysfunction rather than setting healthy boundaries, as the manager's unreasonable behavior was not Emma's responsibility. If Emma had been willing to walk away from the relationship, she could have set that boundary and lived with the consequences, including potential retaliation from the manager. Instead, Emma decided that she wanted to stay in her job due to the impact she was having.

I framed her situation as a choice: Emma could choose to leave the job (and the manager) and find a new one, or she could stay in the job with the consequence that she had to learn to work more effectively with her manager by accepting her as she was. Emma didn't like that choice, and resisted acknowledging it for a couple months. But she eventually confronted the possibility of quitting her job rather than continue dealing with her manager and realized that she did have a choice, even if it wasn't the choice she wanted. Emma had been hoping for a world where she got to keep her job as is, with her manager either magically changing or being removed—but that possibility wasn't happening. Once Emma accepted that reality, she could make a choice from the available options and accept the consequences of that choice. She got unstuck and accepted the agency she did have to work around her manager, rather than waiting for another option to magically appear.

Influencing others—it's not about you

It's not enough to just accept others as they are, because that will still leave you stuck in the same patterns. The rest of this chapter will focus on helping you apply what you have learned to change those patterns more effectively by influencing the people around you to take different actions.

A common frustration for people is that their manager or leader doesn't listen to them. I ask them to describe the interaction, and it is generally something in the form of "I told them to do X, but they said no! Why won't they listen to me and see that X is clearly the right thing to do?"

This was me for the first decade of my career. At one startup, I was so critical of the leadership team that they started calling my cubicle the "Corner of Negativity." It led to a situation where they were making (another) terrible decision, and I wrote a long email explaining to the VPs how it would go poorly. At the end of the email, I said "I know you won't listen to me, so I am only writing this to be able to forward it to you in six months to say I told you so." And then I did, in fact, forward the email six months later with a note of "I told you so." Unsurprisingly, that email did not increase their willingness to listen to me, nor did it improve things at the company (it went bankrupt a year later).

Being right was not enough to change the leaders or the direction of the company. After that experience, I learned to be more effective at communicating my message so that other people would listen to me and make different choices. What did I do differently? I used the simple time-tested wisdom of "it's not about you" to transform the problem from how it affected me to framing it in terms of their interests.

What isn't working for you?

Other people aren't listening to me. I'm clearly right, and they should be able to see why I'm right.

How are you the problem?

When others don't listen, I am stubbornly waiting for them to see "reason." That leaves me stuck because I don't control if and when they will change their perspective.

You have a choice.

Instead of waiting for them to understand my perspective or repeating the same message, I can choose to understand their context better, and take control by doing something different. Perhaps I have information or experiences they don't have, or they have interests or incentives I'm not aware of. Either way, they are more likely to listen if I communicate with their context and interests in mind.

Exercise 4.2

An exercise I offer in these situations is to build a stakeholder map.[6]

1. In your journal, identify the key stakeholders (peers, managers, and executives) that affect your ability to get things done in your organization.

2. Observe them as scientific subjects. Write down the questions they ask and the comments they make at every meeting you attend with them.

3. After the meeting, ask yourself questions like, "Why are they asking or saying that?" and "What might that reveal about what they are prioritizing and what they see as success?" Write down your answers and see if any patterns emerge.

In other words, treat the key stakeholders as the video-game boss I mentioned earlier in this chapter and observe their behavior. Once you understand how they work and think, you can tailor your communication with them based on your understanding of what they actually care about, rather than what you (or your parts) think they should care about. My experience is that when you speak to people in their language, they hear your message more clearly.

---

[6] I first went through this exercise myself at the Amplifying Your Effectiveness conference in 2009, where Esther Derby led us through the process of mapping the influence networks at our organizations.

ACCEPT OTHERS · 83

My typical example is learning to work with salespeople. I used

My typical example is learning to work with salespeople. I used to get frustrated when talking to salespeople because I would tell them about cool new product features, but they were never as excited as I was about what we were building. After having endless discussions with sales leaders about their quotas, I realized their compensation and reputation depended on beating their quota, so that was their primary focus. Once I figured that out, I framed whatever I wanted the sales team to do in terms of how it would help them beat their quota, and they paid much greater attention to what I had to say!

A common question at this point is what to do when you take the time to understand your stakeholders' interests and you realize that their interests and values are not aligned with yours. Guess what? You have a choice.

1. You can leave and find another organization or leadership team who is more aligned with your interests and values. This depends on you having the financial resources and options to do that.

2. You can stay and work within the system. Even if you're not aligned, you will be more effective at influencing others by appealing to their interests, and perhaps you can align them around projects that will improve things. This can also be a temporary choice while you arrange for option 1 of leaving.

3. You can stay and adopt their values, i.e., "go native." You sometimes see this from women who adopt more aggressive, masculine behaviors to rise through the corporate ranks. Or if you're in an investment bank where people aim to maximize their year-end bonuses, you could adopt that mentality for a few years to build up your financial resources. The challenge with this is that people say they'll only do this for a few years, but the longer they stay, the harder it is to leave,

because the values and behaviors become stickier the more that you practice them.

One choice I don't recommend is to perpetuate a broken system. Don't choose option 2 of working within the system when the system is exploiting you. It can feel noble and heroic to just "make it work" despite unreasonable expectations. You don't want to disappoint your coworkers and your manager, so you suck it up and figure out how to get it done. But this just helps to keep the problematic system in place, because the people in charge see no reason to change. From their perspective, they are getting the output they want so the system is working for them; they reap the benefits while you experience the pain. There may be times when you choose option 2 temporarily because of other considerations, but until the problematic aspects of the system are addressed directly, you will be supporting that system's continued existence by sacrificing your own mental and physical health. That's effectively what I did in the role where I burned out at Google, and I do not recommend that experience for you.

They're not hearing what you're saying

Influencing others more effectively also requires understanding how human communication works. You might think that it's straightforward: you communicate something, and the other person understands exactly what you mean. Unfortunately, it's not that simple.

When you say or write something, you are translating your ideas into words and you do that translation based on your experience and knowledge. The listener or reader then takes those words and translates them back into ideas, filtered through their experience and knowledge. That means they often receive something entirely different than what you intended to send, because they selectively focus only on certain parts, or interpret the words differently, or impose a different set of assumptions on them.[7]

When a miscommunication happens, we don't realize how much interpolation both sides are doing. People compare conclusions and then get angry with each other: "Why can't you see reality? It's right there in front of you!"

But it's not. Getting to that conclusion requires agreeing on the specific observations and data that are relevant, interpreting those observations in a certain way, and then picking an action or response based on those observations and interpretations. To diagnose the miscommunication requires painstakingly going through each of these steps to understand the disconnect.[8]

---

[7] Chris Argyris's Ladder of Inference, as described by Rick Ross's article (1994) in *The Fifth Discipline Fieldbook*, is a model that unpacks what can happen even in simple communication:

- Observable reality: We start with what's observable around us in the world, which is an overwhelming number of facts.
- Selected "data": We can't process everything, so we filter and select what we pay attention to, based on our previous experience of what is relevant and important.
- Interpreting the data: Based on our selected set of observations, we interpret our selected observations based on our previous experiences.
- Assumptions: We make assumptions based on the meaning we made of what we observed. These assumptions are often based on the rules imposed by our parts, as discussed in chapter 3.
- Conclusions: We draw conclusions based on our interpretation of our selected facts, as filtered through our assumptions.
- Beliefs: We use those conclusions to reinforce (or occasionally update) our beliefs about the world.
- Actions: We take actions in response to our conclusions and beliefs, mistakenly thinking that we are responding to objective reality.

[8] I once spent three days locked in a room doing a project reset with a cross-functional team, which involved working through communication issues like this. At one point, we spent literally three hours to discover that our frustration with each other was because the engineers, the biologists, and the physicists were each using the word "platform" to mean three completely different things.

When I don't understand somebody's actions, I try to ask myself **"What must be true in their world (but not in mine) that would explain their actions?"** Rather than assuming the other person is incompetent or evil, I assume they are doing the best they can but have a different assumption or experience that explains their actions. Those assumptions or experiences might include:

- They are looking at a different selection of facts than I am.

- They are interpreting those facts differently because they had a different previous experience than me. For example, somebody who has been criticized for any little mistake in the past is going to be hypervigilant about the details, while I might ask "Why are we worried about that detail?" because I have been given the benefit of the doubt due to my privileged identities in the past.

- They have different values or incentives than me, e.g., people will do what gets them the biggest bonus even if it leads to a poorer result for the customer.[9] In Emma's case, she mistakenly assumed that her manager would value championing Emma's success as Emma did for her team, when in fact the manager was more focused on marketing herself.

- Their previous experiences formed a part that believes there's a rule they must follow, e.g., "I can never say no to my manager" or suffering through a miserable job situation because "I'm not a quitter" when they always have the option to leave if they are willing to deal with the consequences of finding a new job.

Learning about these various discrepancies helped me become more effective at communication because I learned to clearly lay out

_____

[9] Mike Daisey (2002) has a great example of this in his book _21 Dog Years: A Cube Dweller's Tale_, in which he describes his experience working as a customer support representative for Amazon. Once he figured out that he was rewarded for spending less time on calls, he started hanging up immediately on every fourth customer, and won an award because his average call time was the lowest in the department.

my assumptions and my data before sharing my conclusions and action recommendations. If somebody didn't agree, I could walk through each step, find the disconnect, and share either the data that convinced me or the experiences I had that guided my interpretation. Sometimes I would have to roll all the way back to my initial observations to find common ground, but once we found a place of agreement, we could move forward step by step to see where our thinking diverged.

Patrick Pichette, the former CFO of Google, similarly looked for key assumptions made by teams requesting funding by asking: "What do I have to believe for this to be successful?". When I first heard him ask that question, I didn't understand what he was looking for. With more experience (and after I saw many poorly thought-out business models), I realized he was asking the team to share their selected data and identify their assumptions so he could see how they arrived at their conclusions before making a decision. By making the team articulate their assumptions, he could also make additional funding contingent on teams validating those assumptions with experiments.

Make clear requests of others

Interacting with others is a series of negotiations where we make a request or offer to somebody, and they can choose to commit to that request or accept that offer.[10] It seems so simple, yet I find it revolutionary to structure communication in that way.

---

[10] Fernando Flores (2012, 29) describes the fundamental unit of work to be a "conversation for action," where one person makes a request of another and they negotiate the terms of the work until the other person agrees to the work. The other person does the work, declares it complete, and then brings it back to the first person for approval; if the work is not approved, they start the cycle over with a new request and negotiation.

The first skill to build is to make clear requests of others. In our day-to-day interactions, most people assume that others "should" know what to do and that they will do the "right" thing, and then get frustrated when what is produced is not what it "should" be. But they never asked for what they wanted! The "shoulds" and "rights" were only in their heads, as described in the previous section of this chapter, and were never communicated to the other person performing the task.

As a wise friend once told me, **"If they have to read your mind for you to get what you want, you're doing it wrong."**

So why don't people make clear requests?

Often, it's because they (their parts) are afraid of rejection. If they make a clear request of "I want this done in this way by this date," and the other person says no, how do they respond or move forward? Most people don't feel comfortable with negotiation, so rather than risk that possibility, they say, "Can you do the thing?" and hope it all works out. Of course, there's a lot of wish fulfillment needed for that to happen; their avoidance generally doesn't remove frustration but merely postpones it until a later date, when the person put in time and effort to do the thing and then is told, "That's not what I wanted!"

Imagine the same scenario from the other person's perspective. Your manager gives you a task. It's not exactly clear what they are looking for, but you work hard on the task, and come back with your best effort. Instead of being thankful for your hard work, they say "That's not what I wanted! Why can't you get it right?"[11] Now you (and your parts) feel angry and resentful that your hard work was not appreciated, so you get defensive and fight back. Not great.

---

[11] I've heard this called the "bring me a rock" game. The manager says, "Bring me a rock!" The employee brings them a rock. "Not that rock, I wanted a rock that is X [adding a new requirement]!" The employee brings another rock that has X. "Not that rock, it needs to have Y!" Repeat until everybody is frustrated.

Note that when you first received the unclear task, you had a choice whether to ask questions about what was expected, but instead chose to accept the task without clarification. In the future, you might decide that you are willing to ask uncomfortable questions of your manager at the start because you have now experienced the frustrating alternative of spending time and effort doing something that wasn't wanted.

The other objection I get is that laying out clear requests is too much work, something like "I don't have time to specify every detail—they should know what I want!" But what generally lurks behind that objection is a part's unwillingness to take responsibility, i.e., if I make an effort to make a clear request, and what's returned is not what I wanted, then I am the one who wasn't good enough. Rather than feel that sense of shame, the part weasels out by being unclear and puts the responsibility on the other person to "get it right."

If we set aside these emotional defense mechanisms, we can see the benefit of spending time up front to clarify requirements by unpacking any assumptions and interpretations. If a task will take somebody many hours to do, and we can spend a few minutes explaining up front exactly what is needed and why, both people will be more satisfied—the requester will more likely get what they want, and the person doing the work will not feel like their time was wasted.

But back to the original objection of "What if the other person says 'no' to my request?" Then they say no. It doesn't mean anything bad has happened to you; even though a fight-or-flight response might be triggered, your survival is not actually at risk. You can decide to reframe the request in terms of something they care about (see the "Influencing Others" section earlier in this chapter), or you can ask what they are willing to do, or you can ask somebody else. Yet many people treat receiving a no as something that must be avoided.[12]

A friend told me a story about somebody whose fear of rejection was holding her back. To develop her emotional resilience to hearing "no," she experimented with making unreasonable requests. Once a day for a month, she asked for something so unreasonable that she felt embarrassed asking for it; in fact, she would preface the request with "I know this request is unreasonable, and I expect you to say no."

The result? Half of her "unreasonable" requests were accepted. Her judgment of what was "unreasonable" was wildly miscalibrated, and it turned out that people were much more willing to help than she expected.

---

[12] This discomfort with receiving a no may be cultural, as described in the article "'Askers' vs. 'Guessers'" (Eichler 2010). East Asian cultures are "Guesser" cultures that use hints and context to guide guests on acceptable behavior, as it is considered rude in those cultures to directly refuse a guest's request. In other more direct "Asker" cultures, people can ask for whatever they want, and the other person is expected to say yes or no. Either culture is self-consistent, but interactions between different cultures can lead to both sides being confused and frustrated. This section will help you to make clear requests as expected in American Asker culture.

Let's use our framework to transform our lack of desired results from a problem to a choice:

What isn't working for you?

Other people don't do what I want them to do. When I ask them to do something, they never give me what I want.

How are you the problem?

I am not making clear requests of others, which leaves both them and me frustrated with the outcome.

You have a choice.

I can decide to make clear requests and deal with the consequences. If I don't get the response I want, I can modify my request.

If my request gets rejected, I will understand they are rejecting only the request, not me. I can find another way to ask for what I want, or find somebody else to ask.

If my parts feel an existential threat from rejection and activate me into fight-or-flight mode, I will use exercise 3.3 to recognize those parts taking over and respond appropriately.

Exercise 4.3

When you are feeling frustrated because your message isn't getting through, here are a couple things you can try based on the previous two sections in this chapter:

1. What do you want the other person to hear or do as a result of your communication? Ask yourself how their behavior would be different if you get what you want. What would be the observable evidence that your communication is received? That is the specific request to make. Here's an example of such a transformation:

    a) "I want my manager to be more supportive."

    b) Ask yourself: What would that look like? What's an example of this behavior that could be recorded on video? Perhaps your answer might be "They would speak up for me in situations where I'm overwhelmed."

    c) Use what you learned to make more specific requests, e.g., asking your manager when feeling overwhelmed: "I would like you to step in and address the concerns of the VP in this interaction." By changing it from a general desire to a specific request, it is much more likely to be fulfilled.

    d) If the request is denied or ignored, you can consider how you might make the request more meaningful to them (how will it help them achieve their goals?), or how else you might get your need met (is there somebody else you can ask?).

    e) You will see another example in the next section where I share the request I made of my VP when I was Chief of Staff.

2. What if the other person doesn't receive what you intend? Then we have to discover where the communication breakdown occurred.

a) Start by laying out your own reasoning.

   i) What problem or issue are you addressing with your communication?

   ii) What specific observations did you make that could be seen by others with a video camera? The video camera restriction forces you to look at the facts, not what is in your own head or what you think others are thinking.

   iii) How did you interpret those observations to get to your conclusion?

   iv) How does your request follow from what you observed?

b) Have a one-on-one conversation with the other person and share your reasoning. I suggest starting the conversation with "This is what I'm seeing" to make it clear this is your perspective and not an objective truth. After you share, ask "What am I missing?" or "Help me understand what you are seeing." By giving them those prompts, you are creating the opportunity to find the common ground, e.g., when you start with "This is the issue I'm addressing," and they immediately interrupt and say, "That issue isn't important, why are you looking at it?", you've found the source of your disagreement and can discuss that discrepancy directly.

Set boundaries

What do you do when somebody is making unclear and unreasonable requests of you, when it seems that nothing you do is ever good enough and everything is your fault?

First of all, breathe. The person making the request is likely dealing with their own parts that formed in response to their experiences and are overreacting to the current situation (it's not about you!). But holding that compassion for them doesn't extend to letting them ruin your life, even if they are your manager or leader. They may continue to use their power to make your working life miserable, but within that reality you can choose whether to:

- Work unreasonable hours to satisfy unreasonable requests.
- Ask to clarify their requests and the desired outputs before beginning work.
- Let their unreasonable expectations affect your sense of self and your assessment of your work. In other words, will you let them make you feel bad?
- Stay in the relationship—if somebody is consistently pushing past your boundaries, then it may be time to consider leaving the situation.

Of course, there are consequences to each of these choices. If your manager is vindictive, they may find a way to fire you or give you a bad performance review in retribution for not doing whatever you are told. As I mentioned before, I received a bad performance review when I told my manager I was no longer going to burn myself out by trying to satisfy their expectations. By setting that boundary, I emerged happier because I chose not to let my manager's desires supersede my own desire to stop working so much, while accepting the consequence that my evaluation and compensation would be affected.

Boundaries are setting limits on what's in our control— which is our own actions. Telling somebody else that their behavior is unacceptable is not setting a boundary, because you are leaving the situation in their control: they can choose whether they will change their behavior in response to your request (kudos to you for making a clear request!).

A boundary is when you commit to doing something differently if the situation does not change, and then following through on that commitment. To use my Google burnout example, I had told my manager that I felt she was giving me too much work. Nothing changed, because she felt the work still had to get done, and it was my job to do the work. Only after I communicated a firm boundary of "I will not work this much anymore" and stopped working nights and weekends did she reduce my workload by giving half my team and responsibilities to another manager. I accepted the consequences of setting that boundary in the form of my manager slashing my performance rating and eliminating the possibility of me being promoted.

The ultimate choice in an unreasonable working environment is whether to stay and accept the toxic consequences to your mental and emotional health, or to leave and accept the consequences of financial uncertainty. In other words, you are making an implicit choice every day when you show up to work. To make that choice explicit, consider what conditions would cause you to quit and accept the consequences of having to find another job. That's your boundary—the circumstances that would cause you to change your actions.

Let's use our framework to transform this common situation of overworking from a circumstance to be endured into a choice:

What isn't working for you?

I have to work weekends because my boss is giving me too much work.

How are you the problem?

When my manager gives me more work than is reasonable, I accept the work and commit to getting it done, even if it means working through the weekend and exhausting myself.

You have a choice.

I can choose how I spend my time. If I don't want to work on the weekends, I can set and communicate that boundary: "If you give me more work than I can finish during the week, I will not sacrifice my weekend time to get it done."

Setting that boundary may have consequences. If my manager responds that I must work weekends or I will get fired, I still have a choice: whether to work weekends to keep this job with this manager or to hold my boundary of not working weekends and accept the consequences of no longer having this job. It's not an easy choice, but it is a choice.

A year into my Chief of Staff job at Google, I was so drained and frustrated that I started to interview outside of Google. Since I was already ready to quit, I took the risk of having a vulnerable conversation with my VP in which I communicated that I didn't like how I was spending my time at work on repetitive operations and processes, even though I "knew" it was part of my job. I asked to spend more of my time on strategic work that would be more impactful for Google and more meaningful for me. I figured the worst possible outcome was that I would get fired and I'd have to look for a new job, but I was already doing that anyway.

To my surprise, my VP agreed to my request. We rewrote my job description to focus more on the strategic work and found other owners of the operational work that had been draining me. Not only did that conversation result in an immediate job satisfaction improvement, I also became more comfortable making direct requests of my VP, which allowed us to continue improving our working relationship over the 6+ years we worked together.

Privilege check: I was able to have that conversation because I had other job options available to me and the financial security to have the time to look for another job. And I had the safety of knowing that my VP shared my demographic (we were both white heterosexual able-bodied men), so I was likely to be judged on my merits, rather than other factors.

If you don't feel similarly safe having such a vulnerable conversation, can you try a smaller, safer experiment? Maybe you could experiment with delivering a lower standard of work if it's being done in the evenings or on weekends, to see what kind of feedback you get. Or perhaps you could volunteer for a project you find energizing and use that commitment to say no to other work you find draining.

Your situation won't change until you change the situation. Building up the courage to take a different action will only happen when you decide that you are no longer willing to endure your present conditions. As a result, you might experience negative consequences and hopefully learn you have the resilience to survive them, as I did after experiencing the consequences of setting a boundary with my manager after burning out. But you might also discover that setting the boundary leads to a much better situation, as happened after my conversation with my VP.

That's what makes it an experiment; you don't know the result, and you are testing the limits of the situation to learn more about your current reality so that you can make different choices in the future that create different results.

Acceptance is not approval, and impact over intent

I have talked about accepting yourself as you are, your parts as they are, and others as they are. You may be feeling tension because you don't want to accept things as they are—you want them to be different!

One helpful concept for me was that acceptance is not approval. Accepting things as they are is merely an acknowledgment that this is the way things are today. It does not mean you approve of the situation or think it should stay that way. But you can't drive effective change unless you start from where things are. If you want to change yourself or others, you must first start by accepting the current reality even (or especially) if you don't approve of it.

A similar tension lies in the social justice phrase "impact over intent." Our actions and words have an impact on others, and a thoughtful person will take responsibility for that impact rather than defend themselves by focusing on their good intent. The reality is that our actions may affect others in unexpected and disproportionate ways, especially when we act from an identity of privilege or authority. We may not agree with or approve of others' interpretations of our actions, but refusing to accept their experience means we have decided to privilege our own interpretations over theirs, denying what they feel and how they are affected.

Instead, we can get curious and explore their experience, perhaps using the skills developed in part 2 of exercise 4.3. What did that person see or hear? What did your actions signify to them? This sort of perspective-taking can be difficult but is a skill that you can develop with practice. Effective change starts by accepting the reality of the impact we have on others, regardless of our intent.

I see these two phrases as the same concept separated by a power differential.

1. When in a lower power position, the phrase that acceptance is not approval allows us to plan effectively within the power structure as it exists today, without necessarily believing in the justice of that power structure. This can include setting effective boundaries, as described in the previous section, and being willing to accept the consequences that might come from challenging that power structure.

2. When in a higher power position, the phrase "impact over intent" reminds us that we must accept the downstream consequences of our actions as reality, even though we cannot predict all of those consequences due to the unpredictable and complex dynamics of causality. We may find it easier to justify our actions by our good intent, but this is a denial of the power and responsibility we bear.

Either way, effective change begins with acceptance of the current reality, even if we would prefer to deny or avoid that reality.

Accept reality

I have now shared how to accept yourself (chapter 2) by accepting your parts (chapter 3) and how to accept others as they are (chapter 4). This theme of acceptance extends to everything else in reality.

In 2020, we dealt with several unprecedented events: the global COVID-19 pandemic, the racial justice protests following the murder of George Floyd, and for us on the West Coast, significant wildfires in California, where it was unsafe to breathe outside and the sky turned orange for several days.

I realized that "It shouldn't be this way" became a common refrain in my brain: I "shouldn't" have to deal with my coaching business slowing down because clients were more concerned about their survival than getting coaching for their personal development. I "shouldn't" have to watch my kid all day because our daycare center closed for several months. I "should" be able to go outside whenever I want.

As you can guess by now, the problem was not the events, but my expectations about the way things "should" be. By choosing to stress out about events that were not in my control, I had two problems: the original event itself and my stress about things not being the way I (my parts) wanted them to be. When I noticed myself stressing out, I started to beat myself up for not demonstrating the equanimity a coach "should" have, and then I had *three* problems. And I would spiral downward from there.

The way to break the spiral is to interrupt it by noticing when we tense up and enter that fight-or-flight mode. That tension is a sign of our parts' resistance to what is happening around us. If we instead pause to ground ourselves and reset our nervous system as described in exercise 3.3, we can let go of the resistance from our parts, let go of our "shoulds," and accept the reality of our circumstances.

Here's a small example of how I practice this: when I recently got caught out in the rain, I instinctively hunched up, and my shoulders went to my ears. My mind started complaining about how unlucky I was to be in the rain. When I noticed that tension and resistance, I relaxed my shoulders and told myself it was just water from the sky. The rain went from being a stressful, unpleasant experience to no big deal, because I closed the gap between expectations and reality by accepting the reality rather than resisting it.

Once again, let's use our framework to transform our frustration with a situation into a choice:

What isn't working for you?

Things are not the way I want them to be.

How are you the problem?

I (my parts) have an idea of how things "should" be, and those expectations are not being met. The problem is not in what's happening, but in my resistance to changing my unrealistic expectations.

You have a choice.

Rather than insisting that things "should" conform to my expectations, I can choose to relax and accept reality as it is. Instead of wasting my energy on resisting reality, I can focus my energy on having my intended impact within the world as it is, and take action to bring the world closer to how I wish it were.

Now we can build from these foundational skills of accepting reality as it is to create different results by experimenting with changing our reality.

Exercise 4.4

You can practice acceptance on a daily basis by changing the temperature in the shower.

1. After you finish washing yourself, turn the temperature down a few degrees.

2. Try to stay present with your experience as the water hits your skin and resist the impulse to jump out, even though it initially feels extremely cold.

3. If you stay present for just a few seconds, your skin and nervous system will quickly adapt to the new "normal." And if you turn the temperature up and down a couple times, you will build awareness that the hard part is not the adaptation but the resistance, the unwillingness to change the temperature and know you will be uncomfortable for a few seconds.

I regularly practice this exercise and find it helpful to build the skill of getting through an initially unpleasant change I know I will enjoy after I start, such as getting in a swimming pool on a hot day, starting a morning run, etc.

CHAPTER 5

Experiment and Learn

---

*Writing is like driving at night in the fog.
You can only see as far as your headlights, but
you can make the whole trip that way.*

—E. L. Doctorow

Doctorow's advice in the quote on the previous page applies just as much to life as to writing. You can't see your whole future clearly laid out for you, but you can still navigate effectively with the limited view you have.

What will your journey be? I can't answer that for you because I don't know what will work for you specifically. Each of you has a different history, a different set of lived experiences that informs your behaviors (and unconscious parts), and a different set of goals. Your path is yours to find, as there is no single path that will work for everybody.

But I can help you answer that question for yourself through the process I am laying out in this book.

First, aim using the principles and exercises in chapter 1 to define what success looks like for you—what do you want to be observably different about your life? You need to pick a direction before you start driving, even if you don't know exactly where you want to go.

Second, assess how you might be keeping yourself stuck in your current situation. In chapters 2 through 4, I showed you how to identify parts or voices that are holding you back internally, including the expectations you have of others. By accepting the current version of yourself and others, you now have a more accurate assessment of how you are making choices (sometimes unconsciously) to prevent change. In other words, you have a clearer picture of where you are starting your journey.

Now it's time to start driving by experimenting with different choices you could make to try to change your life. In this chapter, I describe how to do that by sharing some experiments that can help you explore how to move in your desired direction.

I intentionally use the word "experiment" here because neither of us knows what will work for you until you try it. Think of it as a scientific experiment, in which you have a hypothesis about what might happen, but can only test the hypothesis by trying something different, and gathering data by observing what happens in response.

Calling these actions experiments also positions them as temporary and in the service of learning. If I said, "You should be doing this differently," you might receive that as, "You are doing this wrong!" and get defensive, which would only get you more stuck. Instead, I ask you to design experiments that are safe, small scale, and time bound, so you can try them immediately and see what happens. If it doesn't get the result you want, that's still a success, as you have learned more about what works for you.

After each experiment, pause to reflect on what you learned from it, and then design a next experiment to continue your journey toward the life you desire. Each experiment helps keep you driving in your intended direction through the fog of life.

Exercise 5.1

Let's design your first experiment by starting with what you learned in chapter 2, Accept Yourself, and chapter 3, Accept Your Parts, about the rules that are keeping you constrained in your current situation, and how it feels when your parts take over to enforce those rules.

An experiment you could try is:

1. Write down the actions (and associated rules) that are keeping you stuck in your current situation, in response to "How am I the problem?" You can look back at your answers in exercise 2.1 as a starting point.

2. Explore different possibilities for responding to those situations that are more aligned with the person you aim to be, rather than the currently constrained version of yourself as represented by your parts. Perhaps you can imagine how a person you respect might behave differently in those situations.

3. When you feel the physical signals that indicate your parts are taking over, as discovered in exercise 3.2, try to re-ground yourself through breathing or other actions to reconnect to the present moment.

4. Try a different action based on what you considered in step 2 above, e.g., if the rule was "I can never say no to my manager," perhaps modify it to "I can never say no to my manager unless X, in which case I give myself permission to do Y instead." This is where "You have a choice": an opportunity to experiment by acting differently to see if you get a different result.

Similarly, if your challenge is in how others are keeping you stuck, you can try an experiment based on the exercises in chapter 4, Accept Others, such as:

1. Observe the other person as if you were a scientist observing their behavior as in Exercise 4.2, letting go of your (parts') desires of how they "should" be. Using your observations, come up with a different way of dealing with them that assumes they will not change and will continue to react exactly the way they do today.

2. Make a clearer and more specific request of what you want them to do, as in Exercise 4.3. If they do not agree to your request, communicate each step of your reasoning to find the disconnection so that you can build forward from common ground.

Exercise 5.1 may seem a little abstract, so let me share concrete examples of experiments that have been helpful to my clients. You can skim through this chapter to find the experiments that feel relevant to you, as I have offered a variety of situations in the hopes that a few of them will resonate with your desired direction. Think of this chapter as a menu of experiments, from which you can choose the ones that appeal to you right now and leave the others for other readers (or for a future version of you).

Manage your commitments

One of the most common problems my clients face is being over-committed. They face a classic issue experienced by high performers: when you are effective at getting things done, people bring you more things to do. If you keep adding new commitments without letting go of previous commitments, you will eventually reach your capacity and burn out, no matter how efficient and productive you are. I offer the experiment below to clients experiencing this problem.

What isn't working for you?

Everybody else keeps asking me to do things, and I can't get it all done!

How are you the problem?

I say yes to everything people ask me to do because one of my parts fears that if I say no, I will seem incompetent or uncaring.

You have a choice.

For one week, I will never say yes in the moment to a new commitment. Instead, I will say, "Let me check my other commitments and get back to you tomorrow."

When I offer this experiment to overscheduled people, I ask them to write down each commitment that is being asked of them, and then take a look at the list at the end of the workday. Normally, when they do so, they realize that if they said yes to everything, they would have committed to several days' worth of work, and it's not sustainable to do that every day. In other words, the experiment is designed to illustrate the concept from chapter 2 that you can't do it all. Each individual task seems manageable, but in aggregate, it's too much.

After accepting they can't do everything asked of them, they can try other experiments such as saying no to new commitments until previous commitments are delivered, delegating work, or teaching others to handle some of the commitments they are currently handling. By trying different tactics to reduce their workload and commitments, they learn what works for their situation and can then iteratively design their way to a new approach.

Budget your time

Another exercise I suggest is to compare your priorities with where you are spending your time. I use 100 hours as a baseline of how much time is available to allocate each week, after budgeting around 10 hours each day for sleep and other essential activities. How much of your 100 hours are you spending on your declared priorities?

Answering that question is often a wake-up call for people. They say that family or personal relationships are the most important thing to them, but when they reflect on where their time is going, they see that work comes first before everything else.

With that knowledge, they can design experiments to close the gap between how they currently spend their time and how they want to spend it. This can include:

- Setting better boundaries around work, such as stopping work at a specified time rather than working until "everything" is done.

- Scheduling other buckets before scheduling work time, e.g., family dinners or time with friends. When I was single, it was easy for me to work late because I had no reason to go home. Once I started dating the woman who is now my wife, I wanted to leave work at 6:00 p.m. to spend time with her, and I reprioritized my work accordingly.

- Prioritizing daily exercise. Many top performers schedule exercise before any work responsibilities, as keeping their bodies in shape allows them to keep sustainably performing at high levels.

- Guarding focused thinking time. Many leaders recognize the value of focused thinking time with no interruptions, and block off time for that. For example, former Secretary of State George Shultz told his secretary that only two people could interrupt his thinking time: the president or Shultz's wife (Leonhardt 2017).

- Building in a buffer. Most people schedule 100% of their time, so they have to work extra hours when something unexpected and urgent arises. If this happens regularly (which is almost inevitable in this complex, volatile world), then plan for it! Schedule only 80% of your time and leave 20% available for those unexpected tasks. In the rare week where nothing unexpected appears, you can invest that unscheduled time in building your own capacity and catching up on other backlogged activities.

- Taking a "sick" day. When one client told me he didn't have time to work on a strategic project that had been unfinished for months, I told him to imagine what would happen if he was sick; he said his team would step up and figure out how to cover for him. So, I told him to take a "sick" day that Friday as an experiment to see whether his team could function without him while he took the time for this important, strategic work. If they couldn't work for a single day without him, he would have learned something valuable from the experiment even if he didn't get his project done.

Exercise 5.2

Reflect on the following questions in your journal

Aim: How much of your week would you like to allot to work, to friends, to family, to relaxation, to self-care, and to other activities? Using 100 hours as a baseline makes it easy to assign percentages.

Assess: How are you actually spending your time each week? How much time goes to each of those areas?

1. Compare your answers about how you want to spend your time each week (Aim) with how you actually spend your time (Assess). Where are the biggest misalignments?

2. Pick one misaligned area and consider how you can close the gap between your desired time spent and your actual time spent in that area this week.

Remember that you can't create more time. If you want to spend more time on one area, you have to spend less time on another. What will you give up or let go to enable your intention?

- Be specific: if you want to spend an extra five hours with your family, then plan how to cut five hours of work or whatever you choose to deprioritize.

- Warning: taking the time out of your sleep is rarely a good idea.

This exercise is designed to help you realize we all have the same amount of time, and that our problems with time management are choices:

What isn't working for you?

I don't have enough time to do X.

How are you the problem?

I have made other commitments (conscious and unconscious) and there is no time to do X after I fulfill all of those other commitments.

You have a choice.

If X is a priority for me, I will choose to give up one of my other commitments to make time for it. Otherwise, I will acknowledge that I am choosing not to do X because other things are more important to me. Either way, I will make a conscious choice about how to spend my limited time.

Do the most important thing first

An experiment that combines the first two experiments is to budget your time by committing to do the most important thing first. I love telling the story of the director who explained this to me. He was respected by the leaders of Google up to and including the CEO and CFO because he regularly delivered on critical projects that changed the strategic direction of the company. Yet he somehow also managed to work normal hours at a time when I was regularly working 8:00 a.m. to midnight. I asked him how he did it.

He said, **"I work on the most important thing first. And if I don't get to the second thing, that's okay because it was less important."**

This seems so simple, yet I was failing to do it. I came in each day and spent a couple hours responding to emails. Then I spent several hours in meetings other people had put on my calendar. Then I spent another hour on email, responding to the responses from the morning. By then it was 6:00 p.m., and I had not started on the one thing I had to do that day—which is why I was regularly working until midnight.

My director ignored email that wasn't relevant to his top project. He didn't show up to meetings unless he was critically needed. He annoyed a lot of people who wanted his attention, but he made the conscious decision to focus his time on delivering results to his most valuable stakeholders. He did the most important thing first, and that was how he created so much impact.

Many high performers think that just because they can do something, they should do it, especially if it adds value. But when your time, attention, and energy are limited, there is an opportunity cost if you do something that is of relatively lower value. As an advisor quipped, "Are you doing $80/hour work when you could be doing $8,000/hour work?" The $80/hour work is valuable, but not if it's keeping you from doing the work where you can uniquely create enormous, differentiated value.

Before you commit to doing something, ask yourself, **"Must it be me (and only me), and must it be now?"** Answering this question will help you focus your attention on the most important work you could be doing at that time.

Exercise 5.3

A daily intention practice can help to build this skill of doing the most important thing first.

1. As you start the day, perhaps while in the shower or drinking coffee, take a minute to reflect on what single result would make the day a success. What's the one thing that, if you got it done, would make you feel like you had an impact today?

2. At the end of the day, celebrate if you got the one thing done. If not, reflect on what stopped you from fulfilling your intention. Did you get interrupted with other work? Did you fail to realize how much time other things would take? Did you overestimate how much you could get done in one day?

3. Based on what you learned from your answers in step 2, consider what you will do differently tomorrow to increase your chances of fulfilling your daily intention.

Meet with intention

Meetings are another bane of my clients. As high performers gain greater scope, they spend more time in meetings because more people want their insight and valuable input. When you've spent your entire life being rewarded for sharing your perspective and answers, this can become a trap because your increasing scope as a leader will mean that more and more people want your input, resulting in yet more meetings. This cycle will not change unless you find a different way of handling meetings, as illustrated below by using our framework.

What isn't working for you?

My calendar is full of meetings, and I have to attend because everybody depends on me to provide answers or make decisions because they don't have the necessary context.

How are you the problem?

I derive my value from providing answers. I keep knowledge to myself so that I continue to be needed to provide more and more answers. I like feeling indispensable in that way.

You have a choice.

I can find new ways of providing value. Rather than hoard knowledge, I could give other people the context and owner-ship to understand the situation, make decisions, and move forward without needing me to be present. This would free me up from routine meetings so I could take on bigger and more complex problems.

I once coached an engineering director who admitted that he spoke up regularly at meetings to share his opinion because he thought he was the only one who knew what to do. I asked him to try an experiment to keep quiet, speaking only once at the end of the meeting to summarize.

When he first tried this experiment, his team was alarmed when he didn't jump in with an opinion on every subject because they didn't know what his silence meant, which was an eye-opener for him by itself. He had to start meetings with an announcement that he was trying an experiment to speak less, and that people should proceed as if he weren't there.

He was pleasantly surprised when the team's discussions came to the same decision that he would have recommended. The experiment showed him that he wasn't as essential for meetings as he thought, which freed up more time for him to spend on company-wide cross-functional initiatives where he could have greater impact.

Here are a few experiments I've asked people to try regarding meetings:

1. Make a note of the meetings when you were needed to answer a question or make a decision. For each of those situations, consider what principles you use or what context you have that would allow other people to answer those questions or make those decisions without you. The next time you are in that situation, don't just answer the question, but also share those principles and context. Doing it yourself may be faster in the moment, but sharing will save you time in the future; if they understand your perspective, they can have the meeting without you.[1]

---

[1] Derek Sivers shares a story in his book *Anything You Want* (2021) in the chapter "Delegate or die: the self-employed trap" about how he escaped being the bottleneck when he was running his company. Every time somebody asked him a question, he stopped work and gathered everybody together. He repeated the situation and the question for everyone. Then he answered the question and explained the thought process and philosophy behind his answer. When he finished his explanation, he asked them questions to check their understanding, and had somebody write up the process and answer. Because he chose to prioritize information and context sharing over completing a specific task, his team quickly learned how to handle things themselves, and he was able to move away and let the team handle the company.

2. Consider what you want from each meeting. This experiment was inspired by hearing about the process of Thomas Kurian (now CEO of Google Cloud) when he was at Oracle. Kurian would spend a few minutes in the evening going through each meeting on his calendar the next day and writing down in his notebook the point he wanted to make or the question he wanted to ask at that meeting. When his team saw him pull out his notebook, they knew they needed to pay attention.

   You can do the same, even if you're not in charge. Consider each meeting on your schedule and write down your intention for that meeting. You may realize that you don't even need the meeting, and can send an email or Slack message instead. And if you do go, the meeting will be more focused and impactful because you are bringing an intention, rather than winging it reactively after arriving late from your previous meeting. This can work particularly well when paired with the previous experiment of sharing principles and context.

3. Teach somebody by letting them shadow you. First, run the meeting yourself and have them watch what you do. Then have them run the meeting while you watch so that you can offer feedback to them afterwards on what they missed. Repeat until they run the meeting to your satisfaction, so you can stop attending. Again, this may take more time initially, but this process to free yourself up will allow you to shift your time to more impactful work.[2]

---

[2] This experiment is inspired by Matt Mochary's "Mochary Method Curriculum" for CEOs (2022), in which he recommends onboarding every new hire through this shadow and reverse-shadow process.

Take the next step

I regularly see people freezing with indecision or anxiety when they are not sure what to do next, especially when considering a career change. They don't want to take even one step without knowing whether they are heading down the "right" path. And yet there's no way to evaluate whether a path is "right" for you without exploring that path.

My personal example is dating. For decades, I hated dating because it felt like so much pressure to decide whether somebody was going to be the "right" person for me and for me to demonstrate that I would be the "right" person for them. I felt I had to determine our entire future together within the first date—no wonder that was stressful!

My dating life changed when I realized I didn't have to decide whether somebody was a life partner on the first date; I only had to decide whether I wanted to go on a second date. With that mindset shift, dating became lower pressure and more fun, and I met my now wife a couple years later.

Similarly, you don't have to know whether a new direction is the "right" one for you before you start moving. Just take one step in a direction that seems promising, see what you learn, re-evaluate, and decide if you want to take another step. Repeat.

If you are considering a new life direction, a small concrete step you can take is to have just one conversation with somebody who can provide insight on that direction, perhaps because they are already walking it. At the end of the conversation, ask "Who else should I talk to?" Then decide if you want to have that next conversation, or to take a step on a different path.

Act "as if"

Another common problem I hear from people is that they don't have the "authority" or "voice" to speak up or change things. I used to feel that way myself—that the reason people didn't listen to me was because I wasn't a manager or a leader, and that people would listen to me once I got that promotion. My friends who were promoted into leadership positions firmly rejected that idea; they shared that they got promoted because they stepped up as leaders before they got the formal responsibility. In other words, they acted the part before they got the part, as shown in the example below.

What isn't working for you?

People don't listen to me and don't take me seriously. That would change if I had more experience or got promoted.

How are you the problem?

I am waiting for others to give me permission to speak or act rather than creating that permission for myself.

You have a choice.

Imagine you already have what you have been waiting for: the experience, expertise, promotion, title, or managerial responsibilities. How would you act differently if you had that security? Experiment with acting that way right now rather than silencing yourself because you don't have the "authority" you think you need. Most companies will not promote you until you are already performing at the next level, so acting as if you already have that voice may be the best way to get that promotion.

Privilege check: This experiment is only safe for people with some amount of privilege and psychological safety within their organizations. Women, especially women of color, who speak up without having the backing of an official title or authority may be punished for doing so, because culture has created a stereotype of women as being submissive and deferential, and breaking that stereotype can lead to backlash.

How do you navigate such a situation if you don't have this privilege? It's tricky because without experimentation, you can't figure out how safe it is to speak up, but the consequences of overextending are much larger for those without privilege. This is one way in which privilege manifests itself—somebody that looks like me (a white-passing, able-bodied man) can experiment and any failures will be dismissed as bad luck, but the failures of somebody who doesn't have that privilege will be attributed to their identity, as the following XKCD comic illustrates:

That being said, the way societal and systemic change happens is through people acting as if they have the right to speak or act in a different way. There are risks and consequences of acting that way, and each individual has to choose whether they are willing to live with those consequences. The Black people who sat at lunch counters as part of the 1960s civil rights movement acted as if they had the right to be treated equally, and they were beaten and arrested for their actions. They believed their choice to live "as if" was worth it, and their actions improved things for others.

Only you can choose what potential consequences you are willing to risk in an experiment to live "as if". For some, that might mean very small, safe experiments, while others may be willing to take much bigger risks due to their privilege or other reasons. Either way, recognize the choices you are making and the consequences you are risking rather than letting the circumstances or your position define what choices are available to you.

Use the skills you already have

Another experiment that I offer to aspiring executives is to reframe how their existing skills might apply to a new situation. They earned previous promotions for their domain expertise, whether in engineering or sales or marketing or product, but as an executive, they will be evaluated for how they manage their teams and stakeholders.

In another variation of act "as if," I offer ways for them to map their existing skills to their new executive position:

- For engineers, I suggest thinking of delegation as designing an API, where they specify inputs and outputs and leave it to their team to decide how to get the work done.

- For marketers, I ask them to think about how they would market their marketing team to their peer stakeholders. How can they develop their understanding of their new "customers" and deliver messaging that will resonate?

- For product managers, I suggest treating their product team as the product and thinking of their fellow leaders as users of that product. With that framing, they can gather requirements from their "users" to understand their problems, then design the "product" of their product team to solve those problems.

- For parents, I ask them to think about how they would deal with their children in a similar situation, especially how they would balance supporting their children versus challenging them to learn and grow. When they apply that mindset with their peers or team, it offers new possibilities.

When facing a new situation at work, you can approach it with the following experiment:

What isn't working for you?

I am facing a new situation, and I don't know what to do.

How are you the problem?

Without being given a clear playbook, I am frozen in indecision instead of trying to learn how to handle the new situation.

You have a choice.

I can look at the skills I have and come up with ways to apply those skills to the new situation or ask others who have experience in this situation for their guidance. Then I will come up with specific experiments to test how those possibilities apply to my situation.

Make it an "us" problem

The traditional American school system teaches students to work on their own; collaborating is considered cheating, so students learn to tackle problems as individuals. This carries over into the workplace, where people start as individual contributors who are judged by what they personally deliver.

As most of us progress in our careers, we are asked to take on bigger projects that require us to rely on other people to succeed. Many of us never learned the skills to collaborate in that way because we have been trained for decades to solve problems on our own.

If this describes you, you are also likely to see things primarily from your perspective—a perspective that has brought you great success in the past. But that perspective can also drive a zero-sum mentality that perceives a fixed amount of "success," such that you doing better implies I'm doing worse, as if we were students that are competing for a limited number of available As in a class. This can lead to competitive and blaming behaviors that create an unpleasant and sometimes toxic work environment, where everybody constantly lives in a stressful state of survival threat.

The alternative is to create a sense of "us,"[3] in which you consider yourself part of a team that can create greater success for everyone by working together. Putting the team ahead of your own self-interest means understanding others' perspectives, incentives, and worldviews to build a shared viewpoint and move the project forward. In Google's study of what made teams effective (Google re:Work, n.d.), they found that the most important characteristic was psychological safety, even more so than the quality of the team

---

[3] I'm inspired here by the books *Us: Getting Past You and Me* by Terrence Real (2022) and *The New Psychology of Leadership* (Haslam, Reicher, and Platow 2020).

members. Teams where people felt safe speaking up and taking risks in front of others outperformed other teams where people felt the survival threat I described in the previous paragraph.

If you find yourself getting impatient with others and thinking "Why don't they get it?" or "I can't trust them to do it," you are playing a blame game in which you see your counterpart as a rival. Even if you "win" this interaction, it will damage future collaboration.

Instead, I suggest you sit down with your counterpart, lay out the problem facing the organization, and ask, "How can we address this problem together?" As shown below, this approach creates an "us" in which you are both on the same team facing the problem.[4]

What isn't working for you?

Other people are getting in my way and keeping me from getting things done.

How are you the problem?

I am treating the problems as mine alone to be solved and viewing others as opponents for fear they will benefit more than me if I work with them. I am acting as if we are playing a zero-sum game where rewards are finite.

You have a choice.

Rather than stress about who gets the credit, I can choose to "grow the pie." When we work together as an "us" and build on each other's strengths, we create greater success, and everybody benefits.

---

[4] Note that this is particularly valuable at the executive level, where discussions of engineering vs. product vs. sales vs. finance are not as productive as asking, "How do we grow the company together?" Patrick Lencioni calls this the First Team mindset (Gibson 2011): your peers are your most important team, not the team that reports to you.

Change your language

*Whether you think you can, or you
think you can't, you're right.*

—Henry Ford

The language you use shapes the reality you experience. This may seem like magical thinking, but imagine if you regularly say, "I can't handle that." Repeating that belief will reinforce it in your own brain, and other people who hear it will help you avoid that situation. It can then become something that people handle for you, so your ability to handle it withers away.

When I first started biking, I thought that climbing hills was too hard for me. A couple friends did the Tahoe Death Ride, which involves climbing 15,000 vertical feet over five mountain passes. I thought they were insane, because I believed that riding 10 to 20 miles on flat ground was all I could handle.

Many years later, I decided to start cycling more and challenged myself to ride up the local hill, which was 2,000 vertical feet of climbing. Each time I tried it, I would get a little way up, struggle, and say, "I can't do it," and then turn around and come home, defeated. But each week, I would get a little further. After a few months, I finally made it to the top. I stopped three times to rest, but I did it.

The funny thing is that once I knew I could do it, it became easy. The next time I rode to the top, I did it without stopping, even though I needed 30 minutes of rest the previous time. In fact, it's now several years later, and I only get on my bike a couple times a year but I can still do that climb without stopping. I'm slow, and in far worse shape than I was when I first started trying, but it's never a problem.

Why? Because I know I can do it. Parts of my brain aren't questioning whether I can do it, or beating me up because I'm out of shape. I just get on my bike and ride.

Belief is a self-fulfilling prophecy.[5] If you say to yourself "I can do that," then you figure out how to do it because you won't give up until you get it done, the way I refuse to stop while biking up that hill in my current shape. If you say to yourself "I can't do that," then you will likely quit when you hit adversity, as I did when I first tried that climb.

The magic word I'd like to offer you is "yet." Instead of "I can't do that," say to yourself "I can't do that…yet." This small shift opens the possibility that someday you could do it, if you put in the effort.

Another magic word is "today." We all have days where we're not as energetic or skillful as we'd like to be. "I can't do that…today" allows us to accept the current reality without asserting that we can never do what we want to do.

To be clear, there are times when no amount of language or thinking will change the reality of a situation. But when it comes to our own capabilities as humans, our brains and bodies have far more ability to adapt and grow than we give ourselves credit for. You can take advantage of this by changing the language you use to reinforce the idea that a lack of skill is not permanent, and you can build that skill when you are willing to invest the effort.[6]

---

[5] I did complete the Death Ride in 2015 and it wasn't even hard once I trained for it.

[6] You may recognize this as the language of a growth mindset as described by psychologist Carol Dweck (2016). Dweck also describes a fixed mindset as one that assumes our lack of talents is inborn or genetic. She asserts that a growth mindset leads to more ability to learn new skills because we believe we can grow and change.

Exercise 5.4

Go back to your list of dream options from exercise 1.2, and choose an option; let's call it X. What reactions come up for you when you imagine yourself doing X? Perhaps you hear a part's voice saying "I'm not the kind of person who does X" or "It would be cool, but I could never do X"?

I'd like you to take that statement and add "...yet" or "...today" to it. Say it out loud to yourself in the mirror, putting an emphasis on that last word. How does it feel?

Then ask yourself, "If I were the kind of person who did X, what small thing might I do differently today?" Come up with a few ideas and pick one that feels achievable to try as an experiment. Once you find a small version of X that you can do, you might find that you can quickly change yourself and live into your dream option.

It doesn't have to be this way

I could go on and on with different experiments I have tried myself or shared with clients. If you want more, check out my archive of LinkedIn posts at https://nehrlich.com/linkedin/ as I regularly share ideas and experiments from client sessions.

Hopefully the examples in this chapter will inspire you to translate the gap between your current reality and your desired reality into an experiment that allows you to try something different. As you take different actions, your reality will start to shift around you. Each experiment you try will help you learn more about which actions bring you closer to what you want, and/or whether you want something different than what you thought.

You may be questioning whether you can even try one of these experiments. You may feel that it's impossible to do anything different when you are already feeling so overloaded and stuck.

Remember: you have a choice.

One choice is to keep doing what you have been doing to maintain the life that you have constructed based on your previous experiences and success strategies, the life that your parts have been wired to reinforce.

The other choice is to try an experiment to try something new, to change your actions and see what different results you get. This can be scary! You have learned to live with the results of your current actions. If you take new actions, you don't know what the consequences will be, so it may seem easier to live with the consequences you already know and have accepted.

But if you kept reading this book after I initially asked "How do you feel about your life?", I am assuming you want to make a change. You are growing more aware of the costs of your current choices, and you are growing more uncomfortable with the anxiety or stress of your life but don't feel like you have any other options.

Believe me: your life can be different. Please try an experiment. You can make the experiment as small or safe as you want so it feels manageable or comfortable. Maybe you can try something different with your closest friend, a family member, or a trusted coworker. Maybe you try something different on your own time, outside of work. Maybe you can try one of the experiments I suggested in this chapter.

You may find that there is a better possibility waiting for you, one in which you live life with greater ease and you don't feel like you are fighting yourself, others, and reality on a constant basis. When you accept things as they are, you will be less frustrated and stressed because you've started to take responsibility for controlling what you can control (your actions) rather than waiting passively for things to change.

There is an opportunity cost to continuing to live the way you are. You feel the suffering of your current life and you know the ways you numb yourself or avoid feeling what you're feeling, whether it's through overworking, scrolling on your phone, playing video games, drinking, or something else. You wouldn't be reading this book if you didn't wish your life were different. But nothing will change until you *do* something different. You are part of the problem, and you can change your reality by choosing different actions.

Stop waiting for things to magically change, and take action. Try one experiment. Then, based on what you learn, try another experiment. The magic of experiments is that even if they "fail," you have learned something useful. Perhaps you try something new that you thought you wanted, and you hate it. Great! Now you will be more satisfied with the choices you previously made because you will no longer wonder about the alternative.

If you try different things and pay attention to what works for you and what doesn't, I guarantee your life will improve, because you will be making choices that reflect the life you want to live.

With that control does come responsibility, but it also comes with greater satisfaction and acceptance.

You may feel like a powerless victim who is being tossed around by forces beyond your control. There's a kind of comfort and safety in that feeling, because it means it's not your fault. But the consequence is constantly living in the thrall of others and the events around you.

The path I am suggesting may feel scary, because it means taking responsibility for your life by recognizing that you have control over your own actions. I used to believe that many things were just the way they were and there was nothing I could do to change them, e.g., "I'm just not a social person," "I'm not attractive," "I'm not athletic," etc. Once I started testing those beliefs, I found out none of them were as true as I thought they were. I stepped into a world of new possibilities because I now had the "superpower" that once I committed to do something, I would figure out how to do it.

You can also change your reality when you take responsibility for your choices and run just one experiment to learn how things could be different.

So, what's stopping you? We'll explore that in the next chapter.

CHAPTER 6

Address the Blockers

Courage is the most important of all the virtues, because without courage you can't practice any other virtue consistently. You can practice any virtue erratically, but nothing consistently without courage.

—Maya Angelou

I once talked to Margaret (not her real name), who was stuck in her current role with no opportunities for advancement. She knew she had a lot more to give, but her boss didn't believe in her, preferring for her to keep doing the same things she had been doing for years. Margaret was ready for a new role, and after researching various possibilities and conducting several informational interviews, she had identified the career shift she wanted to make. She customized her resumé for that new role, and saved many job postings that could be a possible fit…but she hadn't applied for a single one. She continued working in her unsatisfying role, hoping something would change so she would feel ready to take the leap.

In the previous chapter, I shared some experiments that you can try to shake things up. But knowing about different possibilities isn't enough. You have to do something different to change your situation.

If you're reading this book, you want to make a change in your life, yet you might not be following through on that decision, much like Margaret. Let's review a few blockers that might be preventing your change:

- **Past You:** You have made commitments and created behavioral rules that served you in the past. Change requires letting go of what previously worked and developing new behaviors to create a New You.

- **Capacity:** You have overcommitted your time and energy in your current situation, leaving no capacity for change.

- **Environment:** You have built an environment around yourself that reinforces your current situation, both the physical space in which you live and the social communities to which you belong.

- **Lack of skill:** You don't know how to do the new thing (yet). Learning new things is hard because it means you have to endure a period of being bad at the new thing, so it seems easier to go back to what you already know how to do.

By identifying these blockers, you can prepare for them and address them directly when they arise. With that knowledge, I hope you will have the courage and conviction to push through the discomfort of letting go of your current behaviors to create the change you seek.

Past You

Changing our sense of self and our identity means letting go of what previously worked for us. Our parts have defined us with rules like "I'm not the person who *ever* lets other people down" or "I am the person who *always* helps others." We built our identity around such rules because they served us in some way, e.g., it feels good to help others.

Those rules were made by a past version of yourself (which I will call Past You) and may no longer be serving you because your circumstances have changed. Helping people is great, but not if you are exhausted and resentful that you are sacrificing your own needs for others. Past You is blocking you from the life you now desire, because you are no longer satisfied with helping others in minor ways, as you have identified new possibilities and dreams for yourself.

To move forward requires letting go of the rules of Past You and designing new rules to create a new identity (which I will call New You).

Changing identities in this way is difficult because our unconscious brain treats change as dangerous—trying something new and different in prehistoric days was likely to get you killed! The instinct to avoid change[1] does not serve us when we stay in a stressful or

---

[1] Kegan and Lahey's book *Immunity to Change* (2009) hypothesizes that our resistance to change is so high that we have a psychological immune system to fight against it.

damaging situation out of fear that something new could be even worse. We need significant motivation to overcome that fear, because keeping what we have feels safer than taking risks to search for something better.[2]

These biases come into play when we consider letting go of a previous identity. We viscerally know how that identity and those behaviors brought us success. We don't yet have the evidence that the new identity and its behaviors will benefit us. It's natural that we will unconsciously resist changing unless we can convince ourselves that the new identity will be significantly better.[3]

But continuing down the path that Past You chose means that the person you are now (Present You) is sacrificing your ability to choose your actions now. Present You is giving responsibility to Past You for your life, which is keeping you stuck. You have a choice—will you let Past You control your life? Or will you make different choices that are a better fit for Present You, while still honoring that Past You made the best choices possible at the time, given what you knew then?

It is common to keep going with a previous behavior, even if the current costs outweigh the benefits, because of the previously invested time and effort; economists call this the Sunk Cost Fallacy (Arkes and Blumer 1985). However, the previous effort has already been spent, so a decision to keep investing should be made only based on the situation as of today—would investing more in this path lead to a positive return?

Similarly, you should evaluate your current situation to decide whether the behaviors of Past You are still serving you, regardless

---

[2] Daniel Kahneman and Amos Tversky (Kahneman 2011) uncovered this loss aversion bias through experiments showing that people feel roughly twice as negative about a loss as they feel positively about an equivalent gain.

[3] A mentor coach once told me that there's only two reasons people change: desperation, because the current situation is no longer manageable, or inspiration, because the new possibility is so enticing.

of how much time and effort you spent developing those skills and habits. Even if there's comfort in "the devil you know," becoming more aware of how your current behaviors cause you stress and anxiety will provide the motivation to try something different. This can be as simple as tuning in to experience what you are feeling in your current situation, as you might be trying to avoid or numb those feelings through productive distractions like overworking and sacrificing for others, or through less useful outlets like social media or alcohol.

Past Me, the physicist

I once let Past Me keep me stuck for seven years.

I read Richard Feynman's book, *Surely You're Joking, Mr. Feynman* (1985) in middle school, and decided that I wanted to be a particle physicist, just like him. MIT was where he went, so I devoted myself to getting admitted there, and applied early because it was my first choice.

I struggled during my freshman year at MIT. I particularly struggled in my physics classes, to the point where I was nearly failing. Meanwhile, I was excelling in the Introduction to Computer Science class with little effort.

At the end of the year, my freshman advisor said, "You're majoring in computer science, right?" I said, "No, I'm majoring in physics." He looked at me like I was an idiot. In fact, he was so concerned that he wrote a letter to my parents telling them to talk me out of my unrealistic expectation that I could successfully major in physics. That annoyed me so much that I committed to be a physics major, no matter what.

Indeed, I was able to recover from that rocky beginning, and I graduated from MIT with a physics degree. I even got accepted into the PhD physics program at Stanford. I wasn't quite ready to go to grad school, so I deferred going to Stanford for a year, and my physics advisor pulled strings to get me an internship at CERN, the European particle accelerator. I would be surrounded by Nobel Prize–winning physicists and doing the work to which I had dedicated my life.

However, I was absolutely miserable at CERN. That was partially because I was a shy introvert who had no idea how to make friends, but I also didn't enjoy the work. My professor spent 40+ hours a week in meetings, and sometimes snuck into the lab late at night so he could do some "real" science. I saw the path laid out ahead for me: 6 to 8 years in a PhD program, 2 to 4 years in a postdoc position to get an associate professorship, 5 to 10 years publishing papers to earn tenure...and at the end of those 15 to 20 years, I'd be going to meetings like this guy? What was I even doing with my life if that was the future I had to look forward to?!

So what did I do? I stayed on the physicist path that my middle-school self had chosen, and I went to Stanford. I was miserable, as expected. I tried to make it work for three years because this was Past Me's plan, and I was not going to quit just because it was hard. In my third year, I didn't study enough for my qualifying exams in what I now realize was an unconscious attempt to get kicked out. Yet I still didn't fail; instead, I earned a "conditional pass" that required me to retake a couple classes.

Fortunately, an MIT friend offered me a programming job that summer. This was 1998 at the height of the dot-com boom when it seemed like every programmer in the Bay Area was making millions of dollars, so I finally accepted that I could make a different choice. I took a leave of absence from Stanford to try the new job, and realized I was much happier once I let go of my previous commitment to be a physicist no matter what.

I sometimes wonder what my life would have looked like if I had just listened to my freshman advisor and given up my dream of being a physicist then, rather than spending seven more years going down that path because I refused to admit I might be wrong. Who knows?

Yet I don't consider that time to have been wasted. While I may not remember any physics, I did learn to consistently think from first principles, and I have applied that skill effectively across multiple domains. You may also have noticed that I use the framework of experiments throughout this book, another remnant of my physics training. I also learned to hold my plans less tightly, admit when Past Me was wrong, and accept reality more quickly. Even the "wrong" path can be a learning and growth experience.

A practical example of evaluating your current situation while letting go of the attachment to a previous investment might be when deciding whether to leave a job. If you are looking at job descriptions and deciding whether to apply, it can be difficult to tell whether you'd really want to leave your job for a new job. One way to evaluate that is to imagine how your current job would be described—if you saw that description among the other options, would it be your top choice? If not, it might be time to consider other options.

Create a New You

You will find it easier to change and let go of Past You if you remind yourself of the benefits of your new identity (New You). One way to do that is to use mantras to remind yourself of who you want to be, e.g., "I am a person who..."

I had a friend who suggested that these mantras were like the operating system of a computer (Andersen 2017), such that swapping them out required low-level intentional programming. She recommends writing a new set of commitments that represent who you want to be and posting them somewhere visible where you can reflect on them multiple times a day (she suggested the bathroom mirror so you could do so while brushing your teeth). I loved that approach and implemented it for myself with mantras including:

- I am generous to myself and others.
- I am curious and look for surprises.
- I look for opportunities to show gratitude and appreciation.
- If something scares me, I try it.

I also found it helpful to regularly journal about how I was doing with regard to these prompts. I would reflect on each mantra and ask myself:

- When did I embody that mantra, even in a small way?
- I would then celebrate those steps forward because celebration helps rewire the brain.[4] The happy feelings reinforce whatever behavior we just did to build that new identity.[5]
- When did I miss an opportunity to act on that mantra? By thinking back on what happened, I could examine what got in the way, which was often a previous rule, e.g., "Don't do things that scare you because they might be unsafe." I would reflect on what I could do differently to act in alignment with the mantra in the future.

The journal also allowed me to track my progress over time. I tend to only look at what I haven't done yet, constantly moving my

---

[4] BJ Fogg shares the importance of celebration for habit formation in his book *Tiny Habits* (2019). He recommends "ABC" to build habits: **A**nchor yourself on a prompt, do the **B**ehavior, then instantly **C**elebrate.

[5] James Clear, in his book *Atomic Habits* (2018), suggests two steps for changing your identity:
  1. Decide the type of person you want to be.
  2. Prove it to yourself with small wins.

criteria for success; once I reach one milestone, I immediately reset to the next one, so that I never reach my goals. But looking back at my journal helped me see when I had made significant progress, such that I was no longer facing the issues I had struggled with a year earlier. Without looking at my journal, I felt as if I had spent the year in a constant struggle with my issues, but looking back helped me realize that I was taking on new issues as the old ones were resolved.

My journal occasionally helped me realize I was still struggling with the same issues, so I had a choice: Did I want to accept Past Me, and learn to work around those issues? Or did I want to commit to a New Me and address those issues more intentionally, perhaps by discussing them with my coach or therapist to identify what was blocking my progress?

If you are similarly struggling to change your behavior, I suggest that you journal to better understand these dynamics. By reflecting daily on missed opportunities to act as New You, you will grow more aware of the circumstances that trigger the emergence of Past You. You will start noticing the signals that indicate Past You is taking over, e.g., the anxiety and stress you feel when there's something that you could do to help, and you're not doing it.

As you practice noticing those signals, you will start to recognize them faster. Instead of only noticing that Past You took over when you journal about it several hours later, you will eventually be able to consciously notice Past You taking over as it happens. And then you can make a different, intentional choice in that moment, one where you ask Past You to step back so you can take action consistent with the New You that you want to be.

Exercise 6.1

Pick something you want to change about yourself, preferably something you have struggled with changing in the past.

1. Describe the habits or rules of Past You that have made it difficult to make this change. What resistance do you feel when you consider the change? Is there a part of yourself that feels at risk? What might you have to let go of to embrace the new possibility?

2. Develop a mantra for how New You would show up, preferably something starting with "I am…"

3. Start each day by reflecting on the intention represented by the New You mantra.

4. Journal at the end of the day on the following questions:

   a) When today did I embody the mantra of New You? What circumstances enabled that embodiment?

   b) When today did I fall back into the patterns of Past You? What circumstances activated the parts that embody Past You? How did it feel when Past You activated in that moment?

   c) What will I do differently tomorrow based on what I learned from answering the above questions?

As you start to practice the behaviors of New You and give up the behaviors of Past You, you may discover that the cost is too high for you to make the change you thought you wanted. That's great! That means you learned something from the experiment: you had a hypothesis that you wanted to change from Past You to New You, you tried it out, and you discovered that the benefits of New You are not enough to compensate for what you lose by giving up Past You.

This can happen when you want the results of New You but don't want to put in the work to get those results. To give a silly example, I used to joke that I wanted to *have run* a marathon, but I didn't want to do the necessary training to run that far.[6] Similarly, when you try acting as New You, you may learn that you're not willing to give up what you gained from being Past You to get the benefits of New You. This is why running these experiments is necessary to map your way forward and learn more about what works for you.

And it's not a binary choice where you either pick a New You or stick with Past You. Your experiments may reveal layers and nuances that weren't visible before you tried something new. You may realize the New You that you aimed for isn't quite what you wanted, but this realization may help you clarify what is important to you; you can adjust your aim to come up with another hypothesis for New You, and try another experiment with what you learned. You might also realize that there are aspects of Past You that still serve you well, and you want to hold onto them. As usual, I want you to realize that "You have a choice" as to who to be, and that the previous choices that led to Past You don't have to constrain you for the rest of your life.

---

[6] Fortunately, after I spent a year training for all-day endurance bike races, I used the fitness from that training to run a marathon that fall, and checked that achievement off my list.

Capacity

Past You has made commitments to various people, and Present You may not have the capacity to deliver on those commitments while also taking on the new experiments and behaviors we have been discussing. That is why the first two experiments in the previous chapter focused on time management and budgeting—until you know where your time is going and you consciously choose new priorities, you might not have the capacity to invest in change.

Energy is another component of capacity. If your situation drains you on a daily basis, it's difficult to generate the activation energy to start something new and overcome the resistance to change. Like managing and budgeting your time, a first step toward change might be reviewing your weekly energy profile to understand which activities energize you and which ones drain you, as you did in exercise 1.3. With that assessment, you can experiment with ways to do fewer of the draining activities and more of the energizing activities so you can generate more energy to invest in change.

I regularly talk to people who want to change their life, but who also say they can't because they are already overwhelmed. But exploring something new doesn't necessarily mean uprooting your whole life to do the new thing.

A good place to start is this: if you're not sure what to do next, **what could you do in 30 minutes this week to learn more about the path?** This is a small enough commitment that you will find time to do it if it is important to you. You may doubt that 30 minutes can make any difference, but creating the capacity to take that first step is critical as a commitment to New You. Each incremental step you take will generate new possibilities that are not visible from your current vantage point, and those steps can compound and create the new life you seek.

Here are a few examples of things you can do in 30 minutes:

- Read articles or blog posts in your desired area to find out more about what it's like to follow that path.

- Research classes and programs that teach the new things to see if there's an option that fits your budget and timeline.

- Find somebody in your network who is already on your desired path, and ask for a 30-minute call or coffee meeting to inquire about what their life is like on a day-to-day basis, and what they wish they had known when they started. At the end of the conversation, ask "Who else should I talk to?" to continue the momentum.

- Ask your network about opportunities for trying the new thing in a low-pressure way. Volunteering at a community or non-profit organization can be a good way to do that, because free help is often appreciated.

My personal example is my journey into coaching. After deciding that I didn't want my life to be defined by a role where my primary responsibility was increasing Google's revenue, I started exploring my values and how I wanted to define my life. But I didn't do anything about it for months, much like Margaret in the story at the start of this chapter.

I did take one step, though, which was to go to a retreat of similarly minded seekers, where I met somebody else who also wanted to change their life. We committed to weekly accountability calls, where we asked each other if we had taken even one action to investigate new options. Answering that question each week helped me identify small, concrete actions I could take to gather more information (e.g., researching a class or talking to somebody who was already a coach) and experiments I could try to learn more about what I wanted (e.g., I started coaching friends and volunteered for a peer-coaching program at work).

Rather than ruminating in anxiety about what could go wrong with changing, I took actions and tried experiments that created forward progress. Within six months, I had identified coaching as my new direction and enrolled in a training program, and my accountability partner had landed an internship at their dream company. Those small initial steps led to dramatic career shifts faster than either of us imagined was possible when we started.

Calling back to my days as a physics student, I think of this in terms of inertia. Newton's first law of motion says that an object at rest stays at rest, and an object in motion stays in motion unless acted upon by an external force. Simply put: if you're stuck, you're likely to stay stuck until you start moving. The first step is to get moving and get inertia working for you, and then use experiments to figure out which way to go.

Exercise 6.2

Let's get you moving!

1. Block off 30 minutes on your calendar each week to focus on your new direction. What current commitment can you relax to create time to explore new possibilities?

2. In the first week, review your "dream options" from exercise 1.2, and pick one of them to explore further. Brainstorm a few different actions you could take in 30 minutes that would allow you to learn more about that option. Use the examples above (research, classes, conversations, volunteering) as a starting point.

3. Each week, do one action on the list. Afterward, reflect on your experience by writing down what you learned and how you feel about the option now. It may help to find an accountability partner so you have somebody to debrief with each week.

4. Each week during your calendar block from step 1, ask yourself whether you want to keep exploring the option you chose in step 2, and if so, repeat step 3. If you instead feel that you've learned what you need to about that option, you can restart with step 2 by choosing a new option and brainstorming ways to explore that option. This habit will help build the skill of exploring new options to help you create more choices for yourself. By starting small, the commitment each week is consistently attainable (Fogg, 2020), and you can invest more time when you feel inspired to do so.

Environment

Even if you create the capacity for change, the physical and social environment around you generally reinforces your current identity, because we default to what our environment makes easy. To change your identity and your actions, it can help to change your environment.

There's a saying, "You are the average of the five people you spend the most time with," so changing who you spend time with can change your sense of what's possible. If you see somebody you know do something, you are more likely to believe that you can do it, too. The famous example is the four-minute mile. Running a four-minute mile was thought to be impossible until Roger Bannister did it—and then several other people did it within a year.

I experienced this myself when I got into cycling. In the spring of 2014, I thought that doing a 40-mile bike ride on flat ground was a major effort. A year later, I was doing 100+ mile rides such as the California Death Ride, which included 15,000 feet of climbing over five mountain passes, and the Leadville Trail 100 Mountain Bike Race, where I spent 11 hours cycling on dirt roads along the top of the Rocky Mountains.[7]

What changed? I started riding with a group of people for whom those were normal rides. After failing to keep up during my first attempt to ride with them, I trained harder so that I could join their group rides twice a week. And once I was riding with them regularly, I realized there was nothing stopping me from doing the races and rides they were doing—so I did. The main blocker had been my own lack of belief.

---

[7] The motto of the Leadville races is "You can do more than you think you can." Since finishing the race in 2015, I regularly use that motto to motivate myself when starting something hard, reminding myself that if I could do Leadville, I can handle whatever I'm facing.

So that's one possibility to help you change: find a new community of people who embody your new desired identity. With that peer support and inspiration, you might find that you can change faster than you would have imagined possible, because your sense of what is "normal" will change by changing the people with whom you spend time.

The same principles apply to our physical environment, which we can redesign to make our intended behaviors easier and our previous default behaviors harder. If you struggle with habitual snacking, you can't rely on constant willpower to eat healthier; it takes much less effort to avoid buying unhealthy snacks in the first place, or to hide them so they are less visible and harder to access than healthier options.

A client who was the CEO of a start-up had built out his team to handle day-to-day problem-solving to give himself time for longer-term strategic thinking. And yet whenever he sat down to do that, he would get distracted by emails or Slack notifications and the hour or two he had set aside to concentrate just evaporated. He realized that he was trying to do this different kind of work on the same computer in the same room as his normal interrupt-driven work. So, he changed his location. When it was time for strategic thinking, he left his computer behind, turned off notifications on his phone, and moved to a different room with a comfortable chair for writing. He got a paper notebook where he wrote down the company issue he wanted to think about and gave himself time to reflect. By changing his physical environment, he trained his body to go into a different mode, and he found that creating that "CEO time" for himself was the most valuable part of his week.

You can do something even simpler. One common experiment I ask of my clients is to take a motto or mantra that we design during a session and post it somewhere visible in their working environment so that they are regularly reminded of it. An example might be "Learning is more important than knowing" for an engineering leader who had built his career on knowing the right answer—that post-it reminds him that he wants to grow and learn more than he wants to show off his knowledge. Another common motto is "Breathe!" because of what we learned in chapter 3: deep breaths reset the nervous system.

Another way you can change your environment that combines both social and physical cues is to find an accountability partner. Because I have a part that can't stand to let other people down, I used that to my advantage by setting up weekly or biweekly calls with a friend. I did this when I was first exploring coaching as I described above, and when I was considering leaving Google to focus on coaching full-time. Having somebody ask me each week "What have you done since we last talked?" helped me keep taking steps and trying experiments each week, which meant I made the shift far faster than I would have if I had relied on my own willpower.

Exercise 6.3

If you are feeling stuck, take a look at your physical environment and the people with whom you spend time. Spend some time reflecting in your journal on the following questions:

1. What changes can I make to my physical environment to make it harder to do what I no longer want to do, and easier to do my desired new behavior?

2. How might the people I spend time with be reinforcing my current situation? Who could I spend more time with to change what I think is possible?

As you tinker with your environment, you will develop a better understanding of what works for you, so that you can take on new challenges.

Skill

Sometimes you know the new action you want to do, but don't know how to do that action. This might not seem like a blocker; there are many ways one can learn how to do something new, including researching online, watching a YouTube video, taking a class, consulting a mentor, or hiring a coach.

But learning the information on how to do the skill is the easy part. The hard part is practicing the skill enough to build it into your unconscious nervous system. You can read books and watch videos about skiing, but none of that will help when you're at the top of a black diamond slope unless you've practiced skiing enough to have the muscle memory to handle the steep descent.

What makes it difficult to practice and build that unconscious excellence? For me, and for a lot of my clients, it's going through the phase of being really bad at the new skill.

In one model of skill acquisition (De Phillips, Berliner, and Cribbin 1960, 69), there are four levels of competence:

1. Unconscious incompetence: unskilled and unaware of your lack of skill

2. Conscious incompetence: unskilled and consciously aware of it

3. Conscious competence: skilled but needing conscious effort and focus to do it

4. Unconscious competence: skilled enough to do it unconsciously with minimal effort

When we are taking on a new identity, we often get to level 2, conscious incompetence, and recoil. It doesn't feel good to be consciously bad at something, especially if you are used to being a highly skilled expert. Rather than experience the discomfort of being unskilled, we give up on the new identity and return to the unconscious competence of our old identity.

Getting through conscious incompetence requires two things: the commitment to keep persevering when you are unskilled and an idea of how to improve. A coach can help with the first by providing accountability and motivation to keep going, and with the second by identifying your weaknesses and prescribing experiments or practices to improve your skills in those areas. This is also the essence of deliberate practice: purposefully pushing beyond your current skill limits by practicing the areas you'd like to improve in. We will talk more about this in the next chapter.

The advantage of committing to effortful practice is that you develop rare and valuable skills[8] that differentiate you from others. While the feeling of incompetence can be a blocker, knowing that it is both temporary and in service of building those skills into your unconscious brain can sometimes motivate you to commit to the necessary regular practice.

This is also why experiments are so important for shifting behavior. Thinking about a new possibility will never change your brain, much like reading books doesn't teach you how to ski, or how Margaret from the start of the chapter was not going to get a new job by waiting until she was ready. You need to take different actions to rewire your brain and build the new skill.

One bonus of learning a new skill like this is that you are also practicing the meta-skill of tolerating level 2 of conscious incompetence, getting more comfortable with being consciously bad at a skill as a step on the way toward building competence. I have noticed that such practice has made it easier for me to try new things that felt scary or dangerous, because I learned that my perception of danger was poorly calibrated. And each time I did this reinforced a new identity that "I can do hard things," making it easier to take on the next challenge.

---

[8] To use Cal Newport's (2012) framing from his book *So Good They Can't Ignore You.*

As you improve at this meta-skill, adding new skills becomes easier, creating an ever-accelerating learning loop[9] and allowing you to expand your skills far beyond what Past You might have imagined possible.

The other meta-skill you will build is addressing blockers to change. You will more quickly identify whether it's Past You, Capacity, Environment, or Skill that is keeping you from making your desired change, and you will develop responses to each blocker. Each time you go through this cycle it will become easier, but the only way to develop this meta-skill is to start by doing it one time. So, pick an experiment, notice what's blocking you, and use what you learned in this chapter to address that blocker!

---

[9] Josh Waitzkin (2008) shares some additional principles of skill acquisition in his book *The Art of Learning*, as he generalizes from his experience of becoming a world-class master in chess, a world champion in the martial art of tai chi chuan, and other areas.

CHAPTER 7

Pay Attention

Attention is the beginning of devotion.
To pay attention, this is our endless and proper work.

—Mary Oliver

Attention is the key skill to build when we are not getting the results we want. Setting an intention to change is not enough, because we must pay attention to notice when we fall back into our previous habits.

This goes back to one of the major themes of this book: "How are you the problem?" Even if we have started doing the experiments we designed to facilitate an intended change, we will sometimes fall back into behavior patterns that no longer serve us. So how do we notice when we stray, and bring ourselves back to our intended actions?

Criticize less, celebrate more

One model I don't recommend is self-criticism. I have a vicious Inner Critic part that tells me I'm a useless idiot whenever I make a mistake. Its intentions are good, trying to keep me safe by always exceeding expectations and never making a mistake. But, like all parts, its methods are childish and often create the conditions it is trying to avoid: I get so fearful of being judged when things go wrong that I make even more mistakes, whereas if I was able to stay calm, I would recover more easily.

This part showed up while I was working on this book. After completing a first draft, I sent it to a few beta readers for feedback, who read it and made lots of comments suggesting ways in which it could be better. Rather than being thankful I had such generous friends helping me improve my writing, I felt each comment as a personal attack on me. I got so defensive and frazzled that I shut down and avoided even looking at the comments or the book for three weeks. The worst part is that the comments were helpful! They showed me where I was unclear and not delivering the value I wanted. But because my Inner Critic interpreted each comment as a mistake that meant I wasn't good enough, it took me several weeks before I could receive them as intended.

I can always do better; that is part of being human. A grandiose part of me may believe that I can be perfect and never make a mistake, but that's not realistic. I will advance faster when I can let go of that perfectionism and accept that I make mistakes[1] and benefit from hearing about them.

The same applies to staying on a new path. My clients regularly get frustrated after we discover some way in which they are holding themselves back, and they identify a desired new behavior they want to employ. They come back a couple weeks later and ask, "Why can't I consistently do the new behavior I want?" These are people who can generally learn and implement new ideas instantly, so they feel intense frustration when they aren't able to meet that standard. I've even had a couple clients ask me to criticize them more so they can make the change faster!

As discussed in the previous chapter, it's not enough to consciously decide to do something; you also have to unlearn the previously adaptive behaviors of Past You, and rewire your unconscious nervous system to consistently do the new response, building the skills of New You. That takes time and patience! You might think that beating yourself up is the way to make that happen, but similar to how parenting has evolved beyond "spare the rod and spoil the child," your nervous system responds better to positive reinforcement.

It makes sense when you think about it. When you say, "No, don't do that!" to your part (or a child or a pet), it feels the negativity and it wants to stop doing that, but it doesn't know what to do instead. By instead celebrating when it does something even

---

[1] Please refer to chapters 2 and 3 if you need refresher tips on how to accept your current self.

vaguely right, it learns to do more of that;[2] in neuroscience terms, the praise reinforces whatever neural connections were just made so that they happen more easily the next time. Rather than stopping the ineffective behavior and having nothing to replace it with, celebration builds the habit of the new desired behavior.

Similarly, when we are walking a new path, we will not avoid "mistakes." It's not realistic to stay focused and act from our intention at all times. The skill to build is paying attention and noticing when we stray from our intention and gently bringing ourselves back to the actions we want to take: intention, attention, action.

This was the insight I had about meditation, which I started practicing as part of my coaching training. While meditation has many spiritual and health benefits, the key skill I learned from it was managing my attention. I focused on my breath, noticed when my attention wandered from my breath, and then gently brought it back to the breath. This wandering happened many times a minute when I started, but the more I practice, the more I'm able to keep my attention on my breath, where I intend it to be. Rather than beating myself up each time I "fail" to keep my attention, I practice the skill of noticing when I am not doing what I intended and then, with compassion, gently bring myself back.[3] Unsurprisingly, this skill is applicable many times a day when I am procrastinating or getting distracted by something.

Meditation can help with moment-to-moment focus, but paying attention to how our actions are drifting from our intention requires a different skill.

---

[2] Celebration is the key to rewiring the nervous system, according to Stanford habit researcher BJ Fogg (2019).

[3] I'm inspired here by David Cain's writings on meditation (2019b), as I first attempted meditation via his online class.

Practice attention through journaling

You can only change your actions when you become consciously aware of them, rather than reacting unconsciously, and journaling can help you build that conscious awareness. By reflecting on when you fall into a certain unconscious reaction, you pay attention to how it happens and learn to notice it faster—from catching it at the end of the day, to catching it an hour or two later, to catching it a few minutes later, to catching it in the moment, to catching the urge before you even do it. Once you become aware of how you are reacting in real time, then you can choose a different action. You once again have a choice.

This process is slow to start, but it's like compound interest. If you invest steadily every day in this growth, it will start accumulating exponentially; change that seemed impossible in the first week will seem natural and easy in a few months.

Exercise 7.1

A daily journaling practice can help you build this skill of noticing when you are not executing on your intention. Please reflect on the following questions, and write down your answers in your journal:

1. When today did I fall back into my old patterns of reaction? What were the circumstances that triggered that regression? What did those reactions feel like in my body?

2. When did I act today from my new intention? What circumstances enabled me to do that?

3. What will I do differently tomorrow with what I learned from answering the questions above?

These are simple questions, yet spending even five minutes each day reflecting on them can accelerate behavior change by helping you to:

- Pay more attention to the circumstances that trigger your previous reactions (Past You), so that you can either avoid them or take active steps to address them.

- Develop greater awareness of how those reactions physically feel in your body, so you can use those as signals to catch yourself falling into those patterns.

- Intentionally create the circumstances that enable acting from your new intention.

- Celebrate the times when you act as you intend, as you start to reinforce the New You identity that says "I am the kind of person who..."

Rather than let an Inner Critic part beat you up and tell you that you can never change, this journaling practice allows you to focus on changing a little bit each day to align with your desired New You, empowering yourself to believe that you can change your actions and develop a different identity. Your answers to question 2 show how you are already acting as New You on occasion, making the identity shift feel more attainable.

One of my clients was an engineering VP in his first executive role. He was a great problem solver and had built a strong engineering team under him in his area of expertise. He wanted coaching because he was struggling to work effectively with his cross-functional partners, especially because he didn't want to "stomp on their turf" or have them question his team. It was an adversarial culture where each VP stuck to their own function and team, and asking questions was seen as a threat.

In our initial chat, I offered the perspective that he and the other VPs were teammates, working together to help the company succeed.[4] Treating his peers as part of his team was a new and threatening idea to him. But I gave him journaling exercises similar to what I shared in exercise 7.1 above so he could practice looking at things from other people's perspectives, and to learn how their actions might make sense given their incentives and experiences.

As part of that, I offered him the mantra "Learning is more important than knowing." That started to shift how he approached conversations with his peers, from wanting to prove he was the expert who knew the answer, to wanting to learn from them how they could work together to help the company succeed. Each time I met with him, we would first celebrate the times when he had lived into his intention to connect and learn, and then we'd consider what he could learn from the times when he fell back into his previous defensive posture.

---

[4] Patrick Lencioni calls this the First Team mindset (Gibson 2011).

A few months later, he came to a session and was frustrated that his fellow VPs were not cooperating with each other, treating each other as enemies when they needed to work together as a single team to get things done for the company. I burst out laughing because he had so completely changed his perspective that he was haranguing them for the very behavior that had brought him to me. Through paying attention to this new perspective, he had completely transformed how he approached his fellow executives in just a few months.

In fact, his mindset shift was noticed by the CEO, and he has since been given increasing responsibilities for companywide initiatives as a result. Even though our coaching wasn't explicitly focused on increasing his scope, he grew his career prospects by letting go of worrying about what others were thinking and instead focusing on what was in his control, which was his mindset and his actions.

That's the magic of paying attention to your own behavior rather than focusing on outcomes that are not directly in your control. Shifting your attention helps you to change yourself in meaningful ways by training your nervous systems to take new actions. And the changes ripple outwards; other people notice your changes and respond differently as a result, changing the world around you.

Deliberate practice

As you learn what is stopping you from getting the results you want, you may discover you need to improve your skills or change your behavior. To grow in that way, you must pay attention to overcome and change the unconscious behaviors that have previously been wired into your brain. That isn't easy! I once complained to my therapist about feeling stretched and uncomfortable when I was trying to learn a new behavior, and she responded, "That is what growth feels like."

Psychologist Carol Dweck uses strength training as an analogy to teach children about adopting a growth mindset where they can learn to do anything. When lifting weights, we push a little harder than feels comfortable, which tears our muscle fibers, allowing them to grow back stronger. The brain is like a muscle in that way—the harder we work the brain with difficult problems, the stronger it gets.

That perspective is supported by psychologist Anders Ericsson's research into how people build world-class mastery in skills, concluding that no amount of natural talent leads to such mastery. Instead, what matters most is a person's willingness to invest in practicing at the uncomfortable edge of their capabilities (Ericsson and Pool 2016). What I love about his research is that it removes the excuse that "I don't have the talent to do that." Even something that would seem to be as inborn as memorization turns out to be trainable—Ericsson (1982) had one of his students with an average memory start practicing, and that student was able to reach world-class levels of performance.

Changing your behavior or building new skills requires practice and feedback. For well-defined activities like memorization or shooting a basketball, drills are simple to devise because it's easy to tell if you've succeeded. For more complex behaviors like those I am discussing in this book, it takes more effort to clearly define what success will look like. To quickly improve your skills requires real-time feedback: what would be immediately observable if you achieved your intention?

This is where a coach or mentor can be highly valuable. They have seen many others build the skill you want to learn, so they can pick out the specific behaviors that need to be practiced, identify "drills" or experiments that will build those behaviors, and offer timely feedback. In the case of the VP that I described earlier, we discussed how to apply his desired mindset of learning to the situations he was facing, and he left each session with concrete actions he could practice to keep building that mindset.

If you don't have such expertise available, you can observe others for guidance. When a new client asks how they can build executive presence or influence, I tell them to think of a leader they've worked with who has the attribute they desire. Then I ask them what they see the leader doing that they don't do—that's the behavior to start practicing. You can do the same thing, and make your practice more effective by asking for explicit feedback from trusted peers,[5] e.g., "I was trying something different in that meeting to create more discussion. What did you think?"

---

[5] I love the *First Round* article "The Best Leaders Are Feedback Magnets—Here's How to Become One" (Berry 2021) for practical advice on gathering feedback.

Exercise 7.2

The key components to improving at any skill are practice and feedback.

1. First, pick the skill you want to improve and break it down to a subskill that can be evaluated in real-time, ideally objectively. If you're not sure of what can be practiced in your desired improvement area, ask somebody with the skill what they practiced to help them improve, or read a book on the subject.[6]

   These subskills may seem insultingly small, yet that is what makes them possible to practice and quickly improve. If the skill you want to improve is public speaking, it has many subcomponents: pace (how fast you speak), energy, volume (not speaking in a monotone), hand movements, facial expressions, eye contact—and that's not even considering the words being said! So don't practice public speaking as a whole; instead, practice each subskill independently until you can do it more naturally and unconsciously. You might practice eye contact in one iteration, practice varying your volume in another iteration, etc.

---

[6] I was surprised at how helpful it was to read Jennie Nash's *Blueprint for a Nonfiction Book* (2022) when I started writing this book. She broke down the book-writing process into clear, simple exercises that helped me quickly improve the structure of this book, in a great example of how consulting a coach can help when learning a new skill such as writing books.

2. Practice that subskill consistently (ideally daily, but at least weekly), and get feedback. That feedback could be from journaling and self-reflection, it could be from a coach or mentor, or it could be from peers or friends whom you ask for such feedback.[7] The faster you get feedback, the faster you can try different things in the next iteration, and the faster you will learn.

I guarantee that if you keep practicing and getting useful feedback, you will improve.

---

[7] Continuing my book writing example, Rob Fitzpatrick's *Write Useful Books* (2021) gave me a structured process for gathering feedback from beta readers to increase the value of this book.

One caveat: We've all heard the advice that "practice makes perfect." Unfortunately, that advice is just wrong; my childhood violin teacher constantly reminded me that what actually happens is that "practice makes permanent." In other words, the more you perform a set of actions, the easier it becomes for the brain to do that pattern of actions, as your skill moves towards level 4 of unconscious competence. So, practice doesn't make perfect; if you are practicing the wrong thing, you are training your brain to automatically and unconsciously do that wrong thing every time.

If you are building a new skill, invest in a class or a coach so that you can make sure you are doing the skill correctly *before* you practice it so much that you make your actions permanent.

One nervous system at a time

We can also change the world around us through how we show up. Humans have evolved to develop an exquisite sense of what other people around us are feeling because everybody is dependent on everybody else in a tribe. If the sentry watching for danger is out of sorts, the whole tribe will experience the consequences, so we tune in to those signals. Therapist Terrence Real explains that our nervous systems were never designed to fully self-regulate: "We all filter our sense of stability and well-being through our connection to others" (2022, 31).

One way this happens is through mirror neurons, which are the neurons that allow us to experience empathy. When we see somebody else experience something, a part of our brain reenacts their experience in ourselves, and this is likely how humans evolved to be adept at reading the nonverbal cues of other humans. This training starts moments after birth, when an infant is completely dependent on their parents for survival, and so learns to interpret these signals to preserve their connection to their caregivers. That early training leads to the creation of part behaviors designed for that childhood environment.[8]

This skill extends far beyond childhood. We constantly pick up on signals from the people around us and mirror their nervous system as a result. We all know people whose very presence exudes calm and warmth, creating an environment where others feel good. We also know people who are jittery and nervous, creating a more anxious feeling in those around them.

In other words, human nervous systems are linked and inter-connected in a web of feedback loops that amplify each other. An anxious, stressed person broadcasts their emotions, which other people pick up on, causing them to get more stressed themselves, which then makes the original person more anxious, and it spirals from there. But when one person can break that cycle by project-ing calm and warmth, they can create a positive feedback loop that influences everybody around them to become calmer.

I heard Deb Dana, a therapist and coach,[9] describe this as lead-ing "one nervous system at a time" (2023). Her point was that we can control only one thing in any situation, which is our own nervous system, through the breathing and acceptance exercises described in chapters 3 and 4. And when we can calm our own nervous system, we create calmness for others around us, allowing them to calm *their* nervous systems. We also become more attuned to those around us, as we pick up what their nervous systems are transmitting.

I'm convinced this is much of what is described as "executive presence." When a person feels calm and confident in a high-pressure or chaotic situation, they calm everybody else down. This is especial-ly effective if they have a position of authority because other people

---

[8] As explained in chapter 3.

[9] Deb Dana is known in coaching circles for popularizing polyvagal theory, which is the understanding of how our nervous system operates in different modes and how we can manage our own nervous systems if we understand those modes. You can learn more at https://www.rhythmofregulation.com/.

pick up their calmness through mirroring, which allows the others to calm themselves down. That is a valuable form of leadership!

See the example below of what a transformation from a stressed to a calm state might look like in this context:

What isn't working for you?

Other people are stressing me out. My manager is demanding too much, my family is complaining, my friends are pushing me to do things, etc.

How are you the problem?

I am experiencing everything in my life as happening *to* me,[10] where I feel like a helpless boat being tossed around by the waves. Between me and my parts, I have made more commitments than I can satisfy, so my nervous system is constantly overloaded. This stress response creates a field of tension, affecting the people around me to feel more stressed, creating a circle of stress that feeds on itself, serving none of us.

You have a choice.

Rather than continue to deny reality, both in terms of my own capacity as well as how others in my life are showing up, I can choose to accept what I am facing. From this place of acceptance, I can ground myself in the present moment, when I am not actually at risk of dying and therefore don't need to be in a fight-or-flight stressed state. By sharing that calm state, I allow others to release their stress without triggering a defensive reaction from me, which allows them to calm their nervous systems.

---

[10] I am using the "to me" language from the Conscious Leadership Group's "4 Ways of Leading" exercise (n.d.) in which "to me" is victim mindset, where I have no control over my circumstances, and "by me" is agency mindset, where I control my actions, aka "You Have a Choice."

To offer a client example, a start-up executive was stressed out about an upcoming product launch that was going to be delayed, because she had committed to the original launch date to the investors and her team and did not want to renege on that commitment. She described feeling a rigidity around the decision, which signaled to me that a part had likely taken over. I asked her to feel where that rigidity showed up in her body. She noticed that her breathing was shallow, and there was tension between her shoulder blades. I asked her to take a few breaths while pulling her shoulders back to expand her chest and deepen her breath and to really focus on squeezing her shoulder blades together.

As she did so, I could sense her shift from a hectic, frazzled state to a calmer, intentional state, as her nervous system released the tension she was feeling.

Less than a minute later, I asked her again about the potential launch delay. She realized that the decision wasn't her responsibility alone, and that she and her team would make the call together. With her calmer nervous system, she could show up as a different leader for her team, one that realized the investors would prefer they delay if it was the right thing for customers. Plus, she now had a tool to reregulate her nervous system when she noticed herself feeling overwhelmed.

She was able to create change "one nervous system at a time," starting with her own. Rather than create tension and stress for her team due to her anxiety, she was able to regulate her own nervous system through the exercise I suggested and re-ground herself to consciously choose the best path forward. In doing so, she created more calm around her, allowing her team to calm down as well so they could make better choices.

Exercise 7.3

You can try a similar process when you feel stressed.[11]

1. Stop rushing to do something about your stress and slow down.

2. Where is the stress showing up in your body? How does it feel?

3. Focus on that physical feeling. What is it doing? Is it staying in one place? Is it moving or changing in any way as you pay attention to it?

4. Can you be with that feeling just as it is?

5. Ask the feeling, "What are you here to teach me?"

If you recall what we discussed in chapter 3, this is another way of working with a part that is taking over and giving it space to share what it's trying to do. You can also try physically stretching or relaxing the part of the body discovered in step 2 above to see if releasing the physical tension changes the situation, as it did for my client.

---

[11] Jim Dethmer of the Conscious Leadership Group shared these questions on The Knowledge Project podcast with Shane Parrish: https://fs.blog/knowledge-project-podcast/jim-dethmer/

Take care of the instrument

To consistently regulate our nervous systems as described in the previous section, we have to take care of ourselves.

Many of us regularly give up sleep to work late or binge-watch a show, or we eat poorly because it's too much effort to eat healthy, or we don't exercise because we're so tired. These behaviors are often a result of our parts following rules that don't serve us, putting us in unhealthy loops.

This book is centered around the idea that "You have a choice." But making a different choice requires both catching yourself in the moment before you unconsciously react *and* having the willpower to do something different from your default behavior. That kind of attention and willpower requires effort, and you won't make a different choice if you are not resourced[12] to stay alert and pay attention. Your body (which includes your mind) is the instrument through which you will make change happen ("one nervous system at a time"), and caring for the instrument is what will enable that change.

If your whole business depended on a single machine, you would maintain it regularly and give it whatever care it needed to make sure it operated as well as it could. Your body is that machine for your life, yet many of us treat our bodies as something we can ignore or override to do what our mind wants to do instead.

That sacrifice can work in the short term! Sometimes we can push our minds and bodies beyond all limits to achieve a goal. I once procrastinated on two semester-long projects in college and managed to get both done in the final week by sleeping only two

---

[12] By resourced, I mean having whatever you need to be the best version of yourself. This includes taking care of your physical needs (such as getting enough sleep, having enough food, staying hydrated) and emotional needs (such as social connection and support) so that you have all the resources you need to focus your attention and energy where you intend.

hours a night. But that was not sustainable; I could only manage that because I knew I could rest after that week was done.

And such a pace does not lead to the conscious, intentional choices I am discussing in this book. When we are tired, we fall back to our unconscious defaults without even noticing. In a study of a parole board that reviewed probation requests (Danziger, Levav, and Avnaim-Pesso 2011), the judges had the best of intentions to review each case on its merits. But their verdicts were surprisingly aligned to the rhythms of their bodies, as they were most likely to approve probation in the morning and right after lunch when they were awake and fueled with food. As the day wore on and the judges got more tired and hungry, they went with the default of denying the probation requests far more often, such that parole was granted 65% of the time at the start of the session and dropped to nearly 0% before a meal break. We may think we are different, but we undoubtedly fall prey to similar effects when our machine is low on fuel.

So, give your body and mind what they need. The habits that I have found to be most essential for my effectiveness are sleeping well, exercising, eating healthy food, and connecting with friends and family.

Sleep is particularly critical for me. When my kid is waking up multiple times in the night, I become a different person. I start losing my temper more quickly as I fall into the victim mindset (everything is happening *to* me), and I lose my capacity to remember that I have a choice. The lack of sleep has compounding effects: I don't want to put in the effort to exercise or to cook something healthy, so then I feel worse because I'm not moving my body and I'm eating crap. And because I feel bad, I might drink whiskey to make myself feel better at night, but that makes my sleep quality worse, which continues the downward spiral.

To break that cycle, I need to remember that "I have a choice," and to start with what I can control, which is my own actions. I am learning to notice when I'm spiraling, and I do something to break the cycle. Exercise is the key for me. When I use my body and get it tired, I sleep better, and when I sleep better, I make better decisions in all parts of my life.

Self-care and taking care of the instrument can feel like a luxury when you are too busy. You can usually skip a day or even a week without noticing any significant impact. But those days add up, and soon you may find that you are not as effective as you once were, and you are trapped in an unhealthy routine where your parts indulge themselves with overworking, overeating, and undersleeping to avoid your current experience of life. And that's the moment when it helps to pay attention, catch your parts in action, and remember that "I have a choice."

Community and accountability

If you want to go fast, go alone.
If you want to go far, go together.

—Proverb of disputed origin (Tolentino, 2016)

It is not easy to stay on this path of personal development, especially by yourself. Every journey is easier with fellow travelers or a community. So how can you effectively enlist others to help you pay attention to when you are falling back into old habits that no longer serve you?

The first step is to find fellow travelers who want what you want. If you have been doing the exercises throughout this book, you now know what you value and how you want to show up. To find others who share those values, it helps to be vulnerable and share what you care about.

Many of us put on various masks to fit in with the others we see around us. But if we all hide behind our socially acceptable masks, we all look the same, and nobody else can tell who wants to be different and how they want to be different. Somebody has to put down their mask first, and it might have to be you. This may feel risky, but the alternative is to continue living with the tension of conforming to those around you.

The easiest way to find others who might share your path is to put your mask down and reveal your authentic self. Putting the mask down means others can find you, but it also means standing out more, and you will likely experience scorn or rejection from people who don't share your values. But they were not your people anyway, and I think it's worth that rejection to find those who do value your authentic self. The reward of such vulnerability is that you might find a community where you can relax and be yourself without the mask.

Privilege check: Putting the mask down and being vulnerable may not be safe for people from historically marginalized populations. Dr. Carey Yazeed, a Black woman behavioral scientist, wrote a devastating critique (2023) of how Brené Brown's advice to be vulnerable does not work for Black women because they will be judged and punished for showing up vulnerably, making it unsafe to do so. In such situations, you need to assess the safety of the environment by looking for evidence that other people who look like you can be themselves without suffering undue consequences. Without such evidence, the risks are much higher, and you might need more assurance that it will be safe before putting down the mask.

Once you find those who are aligned with you, then staying on the path becomes easier:

1. You have role models who demonstrate the behaviors and choices you want to make, so you can be motivated by seeing the results of living that life.

2. You have accountability partners who will tell you when you're not showing up in the way you said you would.

Regarding the second point, you can choose to make a public commitment to the behavior you want to display. By making that commitment, you are empowering others to hold you accountable to that behavior and can even explicitly ask them to let you know when you are not living up to those standards. This gets them invested in your success, includes them on your path, and allows you to share the burden of monitoring and regulating yourself.

When you do fall short of your desired behavior as we all do sometimes, you will be able to talk about it without judgment in such a community. Other people who are walking or have walked a similar path will understand and sympathize when you struggle, because they have been through similar struggles. And they will gently nudge you back by acting as role models and helping you reregulate your nervous system by talking you through options to recover.

One caution: Because of our powerful need for belonging, it is critical to choose communities that are aligned with your values. Otherwise, social pressures can easily lead you into making choices you didn't intend to make, a tendency that cult leaders exploit. But when you do find your fellow travelers, it creates greater ease and joy in the journey itself. It's worth repeating the saying "You are the average of the five people you spend the most time with"—your companions will bias you to become more like them, so choose them intentionally.

* * *

In this chapter, I've shared some practices and mechanisms that can help you pay attention and stay on the path you have chosen. But none of these will work unless you commit to that path and choose actions on that path each day. The only thing you control is your next action—so what will you choose?

When I first meet a potential coaching client, I always share a disclaimer that nothing will change as a result of our conversations unless they change their own behavior between sessions. I can offer alternatives, I can share frameworks, I can talk until I'm blue in the face, but nothing will change for them unless they decide to put what we've talked about into action and pay attention to make different choices than the ones they made in the past.

The same disclaimer applies to this book. I have shared the simple (but not easy!) mindsets and practices that helped me and my clients change our lives. But nothing will change in your life unless you take these ideas and put them into practice. This may be challenging, as you have likely built an environment around yourself that reinforces your current identity, including your internal voices (parts), your friends, your peers, and even your physical environment. But by applying the ideas in the previous two chapters, you can start building a new environment for a new identity that empowers you to take action on your dreams.

CHAPTER 8

Aspire

---

*To commit to something you could actually accomplish is such
small potatoes for a lofty, sacred human being like yourself.*

—Norman Fischer, *Training in Compassion*

*You have to act as if it were possible to radically transform
the world. And you have to do it all the time.*

—Angela Davis

In chapter 1, we imagined a different possibility for our lives, one where we felt more energized, got more of our emotional needs met by our day-to-day activities, and chose our actions based on our present selves rather than past decisions. We used those exercises as an aiming point for our work in the next several chapters, where we developed the skills of accepting the current reality of ourselves and others, of experimenting to learn how to move ourselves toward that possibility, and of staying on the new path by addressing likely blockers and paying attention.

With those skills, we can aspire toward a greater purpose and meaning for our lives, one that is about more than surviving each day and fulfilling the expectations created for us by others. Now we can think bigger, moving beyond creating a satisfying life for ourselves to thinking about how we can have more impact and even change the world.[1]

Making mistakes is part of growth

I used to think mistakes were bad. I feared that making a mistake would show that I wasn't good enough or smart enough, so I only took on work that I *knew* I could deliver to perfection.

After one job ended poorly, I had a mentor ask me what mistakes I had made, and I proudly answered that I hadn't made any major mistakes. He looked at me sadly and said, "If you're not making a catastrophic mistake at work at least once or twice a year, you're not pushing hard enough!"

That made no sense to me at the time. I had always prided myself on having the right answer and getting 100% on tests, so I didn't comprehend the idea that making mistakes could be a good thing.

---

[1] I love the subtitle of Nilofer Merchant's (2017) book *The Power of Onlyness*: "Make Your Wild Ideas Mighty Enough to Dent the World." This chapter is about finding those wild ideas that will put a dent in the world.

His point was that being so reluctant to make a mistake also meant I was playing it too safe. I had no idea what my capabilities were because I never tested them for fear of going over the edge. To grow and learn faster, I needed to be willing to risk more.

Privilege check: My mentor as a white man and me as a white-passing man have more scope to make mistakes than women or people of color, for whom a mistake can be used to justify a bias that they can't be trusted to handle the work. I've heard from multiple people of color how their performance review was headlined by one small mistake overriding all the impactful work they had done over the year. This advice to embrace making mistakes to find the limits of your capabilities is far riskier if you experience prejudice in that way, and is yet another reason why anybody who isn't a white male is at a disadvantage in accelerating their career like this. Note that my own reluctance to test my limits was likely due to being raised by my Korean mother, as she had probably experienced that bias herself.

I was limiting my impact by only committing to well-defined projects with clear paths to delivering the desired results. Those conservative commitments appeased the part of me that wanted to avoid mistakes in the hope of staying safe, but they had an opportunity cost: I didn't spend my time on more ambitious (and riskier!) projects that could have accelerated my growth and created more impact. This became clear to me as I watched my friends' careers accelerate past mine, as they started companies and took leaps into undefined territory.

I realized that trying to avoid mistakes was too low a bar for myself, because that meant I was limiting myself to activities where I already knew I could reach that "perfection" by following a well-established path.

I now aspire to *more* than such perfection. I am willing to embrace the mistakes and setbacks that come with exploring unknown territory,[2] so I can move beyond the paths others have created and create new possibilities that can change the world. I do this knowing that such an ambition is inherently improbable, and that I can't expect to achieve that result.

Yet people change the world all the time. How? By getting up each day, focusing on what they can control, and acting to move things toward their intentions. If they consistently do that, others may see them as role models and start following their lead. One person's aspiration can inspire another person, who inspires another person, and if enough people join that aspiration, the world changes.

Act from a future possibility

You may have heard of the butterfly effect as an illustration of complexity dynamics, where a butterfly flapping its wings can potentially create a tornado on the other side of the world.

In other words, the smallest of actions can have disproportionately large ripple effects. Since we can never predict how our actions might affect other things in a complex, interconnected world, any action could have disproportionate power and meaning. I can never know when I might be that butterfly; somebody who sees me as a role model could be watching and they might take a different action as a result of seeing me act.

With that mindset, changing the world starts with choosing your actions to consciously live in the world you wish to bring into

---

[2] I am reminded here of Layla Saad's exhortation in *Me and White Supremacy* (2020, 167): "You *will* be called out/in as you do antiracism work. Making mistakes is how you learn and do better going forward. Being called out/in is not a deterrent to the work. It is part of the work. And there is no safety in this work. There has been no safety for BIPOC under white supremacy."

existence. Your actions will demonstrate that one can live in that possible future world today—and invite others to join you in that world. Each person you inspire to act differently is another vote for that future possibility, and that's how you can become the butterfly that changes the world.

Every major social change is a result of brave souls acting as if their future world could come into existence. Here are a few examples of such inspirational actions:

- During the civil rights movement of the 1960s, Black people acted as if they deserved to sit where they wanted regardless of their skin color. The first ones who did so were punished through beatings and imprisonment, but their commitment to continuing to act as if they had the rights that are specified in the US Constitution eventually led to progress, even if there still is a long way to go towards eliminating racism. Black Lives Matter is a current movement working to close that gap.

- Behind the Iron Curtain in Eastern Europe in the mid-twentieth century, the resistance had no way to fight the military power of the Soviet Union. In his essay "The Power of the Powerless," Vaclav Havel (1985) advocated for people to "live within the truth" and stop accepting and reinforcing the lies being told by the totalitarian Communist government. He was imprisoned as a result, but "living in truth" inspired others trying to subvert and overthrow the Communist empire in Europe, a result that was eventually achieved in 1989.

- Activists have drastically shifted LGBTQ+ acceptance within my lifetime. As a kid in the 1980s, homosexuality was still a taboo topic and was rarely recognized in mass media or culture. When a few of my college housemates shared that they were gay, I was extremely uncomfortable because I had no experience or contact with homosexuality as part of my suburban upbringing. But I quickly learned that they were just people and there was nothing to fear. It took courage to be themselves, despite my reaction. In the 1990s, that discomfort was common enough that gay marriage was considered too threatening to ever be a realistic political possibility. But LGBTQ+ people kept coming out and living their lives despite the very real threat of discrimination or violence, and their courage led to a huge cultural shift in just a few decades, though there is still far to go.

- In a business context, every new company starts with a group of people acting "as if." The founders have a vision of how the world can be different, and when they start out, their aspirations may seem unrealistic and even laughable. But their enthusiasm and conviction attract others to join them, and their work together can grow companies to become world-changing forces.

Taking on such a project to change the world is not about the outcome because you will rarely see immediate results. It is about believing so strongly in your vision of the future and your own values that you act in the present to bring it into existence.

Who will you serve?

How do you keep sustaining your belief in a future possibility when it seems distant and unattainable? I believe it starts by identifying who you will serve and who you will fight for even against impossible odds.

I started this book by asking how you felt about your life. There's an increasing amount of research showing that what makes a life satisfying is feeling connected to something bigger than yourself, having a purpose or meaning beyond your own welfare.[3] We can find this connection in a myriad of ways, from becoming a parent, to teaching or mentoring others, to serving our community. Working with others toward a common cause is more satisfying because we share our experiences and become part of a greater whole together, much like humans once lived together in tribes.

Choosing a cause or community bigger than yourself can also help you envision the future you want to build in which that community is thriving. With that clarity, you can start trying experiments in the present to help your community move towards that future. Each action you take in alignment with that purpose is an opportunity to inspire others to join you in bringing that future into existence.

A commitment to your chosen community will provide direction, purpose, and meaning to your daily actions, reducing the need for external feedback or validation. Your values will let you evaluate the meaning of your actions in the moment because you will know that actions taken to benefit the community have value in and of themselves, regardless of the immediate results. And if you don't get your desired results, you won't give up, but will instead learn from what happened and try again.

Let's consider the alternative: If you live your life only to achieve some desired future results, you are giving up present-day satisfaction for the sake of an uncertain outcome, because we live in a complex and volatile world. If you sacrificed your values or integrity or your relationships in anticipation of those results and then don't get them, how would you feel?

To make it more concrete, let's imagine you wanted to earn more for your family, so you worked long hours, traveled regularly,

---

[3] Murthy (2020) and Hari (2018) summarize this research. I also like the expression of this idea in Viktor Frankl's book *Man's Search for Meaning* (1946), where he shares how he created meaning in the suffering he experienced in the Nazi concentration camps by reminding himself of his love for his wife and the meaning he found in his psychological research.

and were never home to see your kids because you "had to" do what was necessary to get a promotion. But then the company hit hard times and laid you off instead. So, you sacrificed your relationship with your partner and kids for the sake of an outcome you didn't even get. That would feel horrific, yet is all too common a story.

Instead, you can live a meaningful life in the present moment by aligning how you spend your time and attention with the people who matter most to you. If you put their welfare first, you will act with integrity regardless of the outcomes you get. Committing to serve others in this way is how you develop the steadfast willpower to keep pushing for change even in difficult or impossible circumstances. And as demonstrated by the activists I mentioned in the previous section, sometimes that steadfast commitment can even change the world.

My aspiration of connection

To make this talk of aspiration and commitment more concrete, let me share my own aspiration. I read a couple books in the fall of 2022 describing how we are growing more disconnected as a society,[4] which felt especially poignant after the loneliness induced by the COVID-19 pandemic. Reading those books crystallized that

---

[4] In his book *Together*, Dr. Vivek Murthy says "So many of the problems we face as a society—from addiction and violence to disengagement among workers and students to political polarization—are worsened by loneliness and disconnection. Building a more connected world holds the key to solving these and many more of the personal and societal problems confronting us today" (2020, xix).

In his book *Lost Connections*, Johann Hari says "When we talk about home today, we mean just our four walls and (if we're lucky) our nuclear family. But that's never been what home has meant to any humans before us. To them, it meant a community—a dense web of people all around us, a tribe. But that is largely gone. Our sense of home has shriveled so far and so fast it no longer meets our need for a sense of belonging. So, we are homesick even when we are at home" (2018, 98).

I was feeling especially lonely and disconnected myself, as the necessity of pandemic-related isolation had intersected with me losing my work community after becoming self-employed as a coach. That loneliness was amplified by the intensity of being a parent of two young children in pandemic times.

Connection is something I have cared about for decades, as I have always craved a sense of belonging. Through my personal development, I learned that such belonging starts with accepting myself (the subject of chapters 2 and 3). Once I realized that others are similarly craving acceptance and connection, I knew I could invest myself in building connection without concern that my effort would be wasted.

Beyond that, I am energized when I seek and find connection. Connection is so motivating for me that I left a lucrative job at Google to build an independent coaching practice because coaching people creates that meaningful connection I seek. I am not doing this work to get somewhere else, always seeking some future outcome and never satisfied with where I am. Instead, my coaching work brings me energy and joy in the present moment.

Using connection as my aim has led me in unexpected directions in the past year. Both Vivek Murthy and Johann Hari suggested in their books that people could counteract loneliness and build connection by getting more involved in their local community. In the month after I read their books, I saw two possibilities to do just that: somebody posted on my neighborhood mailing list that my local city council was looking for citizen volunteers to serve on advisory boards, and I met an executive director of a nonprofit whose organization partnered with local nonprofits and emphasized building a community of givers who are learning together to drive effective change.

Past Me might have said "oh, that's interesting," and moved on without thinking about it because "that's not what I do" or because it wouldn't help me advance my career.

Instead, I followed up on both opportunities. I am now on the local library's board of trustees, meeting monthly with the library leadership team to consider how to better serve our community. I also donated to the nonprofit and am going to monthly events where we learn from our community partners about how we can serve them, and work together to help those partners increase their impact.

I've also been looking for more opportunities to convene and connect others by organizing discussions on topics such as being a woman leader in tech, figuring out what's next when you reach the top of the career ladder as a VP, and becoming a new coach and starting your own business.

Past Me would have said I was a shy introvert who would find such social organizing too stressful to manage. But I now recognize that inner voice as one of my parts that was trying to keep me safe. Reading those books after two years of pandemic isolation convinced me that connection was more important to me than safety.

Bringing it all together, I used the process outlined in this book to find a new path:

- **Aim:** I wanted to become more connected with others and to be less lonely. I set my mantra for 2023 to be "Connect with courage and vulnerability."

- **Accept how I was the problem:** I was depending on others for connection; I waited for others to initiate contact with me and blamed them if I felt lonely. I was letting my parts limit what was possible by convincing me I couldn't reach out to others or try something new because I might get rejected or fail.

- **Pay Attention:** I look for opportunities to connect with people in new ways and actively follow up on such opportunities.

- **Experiment** with making different choices: I am currently trying several experiments to create more connection, including writing this book. It's too early to evaluate what will "work," but I feel empowered to keep trying more experiments because connection is important enough to me that I am willing to accept repeated "failure."

Connection has become my aspiration, the lofty commitment I am willing to make because it resonates on so many levels for me, including:

- Connecting with myself and my parts with more love and acceptance
- Connecting with my family and my friends to share similar love and acceptance
- Connecting my clients with their aspirations, helping them let go of their past identities and embrace future possibilities
- Connecting with my community because humans are designed to live in tribes where we support each other

I also discovered that this aspirational mindset lowered my anxiety because I was not evaluating myself based on day-to-day results. I feel that every connection attempt is worthwhile regardless of the result. Rather than wasting energy beating myself up when I fail to connect, I accept the new information as a learning about myself or others, and I come up with a new experiment to try.

Without that fear of failure, I see more opportunities to connect because I'm paying attention in a different way. Instead of dismissing a new possibility with thoughts like "I don't know how to do that" or "that's not who I am" (letting Past Me or my parts decide), I use my present intention to choose actions that reflect the more connected future I want to inhabit.

To think even bigger, connection is what is missing in American society, as our culture becomes more partisan and dysfunctional each year. We focus on what separates us from each other, rather than the common humanity that connects us. That feels like too big a problem for any one individual to tackle, and it is.

But remember the butterfly analogy. I don't have to solve the whole problem. I just have to take actions each day that align with the connection mindset. With the principles of this book in mind, I can show up with a calm energy because I accept myself as I am, and I accept others as they are. From that place of acceptance, I look for ways I can connect with others and create a future together, one nervous system at a time.

Though I do not often fulfill this lofty commitment to connection, I celebrate the moments each week when I feel that connection with others. Those moments inspire me to keep learning and growing and practicing so I can live into that aspiration. And I have heard from others that they are inspired by my commitment to connection and are taking their own actions that mirror that commitment. I am starting to change the world from where I am.

Exercise 8.1

Now it's time for you to explore possibilities for your own aspiration. Here are a few starting points:

- Calling back to exercise 1.3, what are you energized by? An aspiration that doesn't connect you to energy and flow is unlikely to be sustainable for you.

- Who or what will you continue to value in the future? One way to answer this question is to look back at yourself five or ten years ago: what did you care about then, and what still resonates today? If there is something you have believed in strongly for years or a community that continues to be important to you, then investing your time and attention in that area or community will likely continue to be meaningful to you for the foreseeable future,[5] as connection is for me.

- What do you want to be remembered for? Imagine that you are at your funeral, and somebody is memorializing your life. What difference would you like to have made? Who would you like to have helped or been a role model for?

Based on your answers, try an experiment to see what each of these possibilities feels like, to help somebody in a community or advance a cause you care about. What is the smallest action you can take that might represent one of these possibilities?

---

[5] I'm inspired here by Jeff Bezos, who once commented, "I almost never get the question: 'What's not going to change in the next 10 years?'…When you have something that you know is true, even over the long term, you can afford to put a lot of energy into it." (Haden, 2017) In the case of Amazon, he trusted that customers will always want lower prices and faster delivery, so he could invest vast resources into those areas without worrying he would regret that decision. Similarly, a cause or community that you have cared about for years is one to which you can make a long-term aspirational commitment.

For instance, if you are considering education as a possibility, you don't have to change the education system as your first step; instead, tutor one child. If it feels good, take the next step, described in chapter 5 as an experiment.

An aspiration will resonate with you and inspire you to do more. You will feel energized and empowered, such that you can hold both the messy reality of the present and an inspiring vision of the future.

I also want to note that an aspiration doesn't have to look like a huge world-changing possibility. Being a great parent or partner could be your aspiration and might be what you want to be re-membered for in life. And that's great! If you are energized by that role, living into it fully would bring that energy to all those who interact with you. And who knows what effect that energy might bring to your community?

Follow your aspiration

Find out who you are, and do it on purpose.

— Dolly Parton

Finding and following your aspiration will be a journey where you apply the skills you learned in this book, starting with aiming yourself based on who you want to serve, assessing and accepting what is keeping you from serving them today, and experimenting to learn how to more effectively serve them sustainably with energy and joy.

When you go on this journey and seek your aspiration by applying the principles of this book, you will learn why you are here and who you are serving. You will find more energy and aliveness by consciously choosing your actions with purpose, thus taking responsibility for your life. You will spend less time in anxiety and doubt because you will be living in integrity[6] with your values rather than questioning yourself or holding onto your doubts. You will show up with your whole self and your full energy in each moment, and people will feel the qualitative difference in your presence as a result.

A VP at a pre-IPO start-up once considered hiring me as a coach. Toward the end of our initial chat, he asked me, "Are you satisfied with your life?" and I said, "Yes, absolutely!" without thinking.

We both paused in shock—him because he couldn't imagine such peace despite his many accomplishments, and me because I had never been able to say that without caveats before. It was a

---

[6] I love Katie Hendricks's definition of integrity as "energetic wholeness" (2022) When you live from integrity, you are not losing energy to doubt and anxiety or wasting energy on unspoken resentments, unkept agreements, or unfelt feelings, and thus are able to show up with your full self in each moment.

crystallizing moment for me in realizing why I loved the work of coaching: I had found a purpose where I could be satisfied with my life in the moment, regardless of the outcome.

That is what it feels like to live in integrity. That is what it feels like to choose one's actions each day to align with one's values and aspirations. It took me years to reach this point, and I wrote this book as a guide to help you get there, too.

Please join me and become a butterfly that creates positive change. The world will be a better place if more people find and connect to their aspirations in this way. I hope that you can aim in a purposeful direction, accept yourself and others, and experiment your way toward finding meaning and purpose in your life. May your journey start today.

Acknowledgments

I would like to thank the following people:

Vik Gupta, for telling me to think bigger and write a book to share my own ideas, rather than constantly referencing other people's books.

James Flaherty, Anamaria Aristizabal, and Kristin Cobble, as the coaches who led me through my transformation into the coaching way of being in the Professional Coaching Course of New Ventures West.

Steve March, whose Aletheia Coaching methodology, also called Integral Unfoldment, introduced me to the language of parts and Internal Family Systems, and whose teachings across the four depths of Parts, Process, Presence, and Nonduality significantly accelerated my personal development while also increasing my coaching skills.

Jerry Colonna, for demonstrating compassionate, insightful coaching on the Reboot podcast.

Jerry Weinberg, for his pioneering insight that "no matter what they say, it's always a people problem." He blazed a path for me to follow as a generalist, and I was privileged to attend one of the last of his legendary Problem Solving Leadership workshops in 2015 before he passed away in 2018.

Jim Dethmer and Diana Chapman of the Conscious Leadership Group, especially for sharing the framework of "to me/by me/through me/as me" consciousness. This book is a guide to help people move out of "to me" victim consciousness by recognizing they have the choice to author their lives as they intend ("by me").

My mentors, Jon Williams and Sanjay Datta, who challenged me to let go of my limiting beliefs and gave me valuable advice that I sometimes didn't understand until years later.

Jennie Nash, for her book *Blueprint for a Nonfiction Book*. Her exercises helped me clarify my intent in writing this book and to get started with, well, a blueprint. She also generously gave her feedback on an early draft of the introduction chapter, pressing me to find my own voice as a writer.

Rob Fitzpatrick, for his book *Write Useful Books* that convinced me to share my chapter drafts with beta readers to get early feedback on the usefulness of what I was writing.

Seppo Helava, for being my accountability partner as we pushed each other to write our books.

Jenn Steele, for being a thought partner as I explored many of these ideas.

My beta readers, who read several versions of this book and provided feedback to make each draft better: Rathna Thiyagarajan, Seppo Helava, Jessica Forbess, Jessica Fan, and Adam Birnbaum.

My clients, from whom I have learned so much. I'd especially like to thank the clients who generously agreed to share their stories in this book and offered encouragement on early drafts.

Saeah, Amy, and the Otterpine team for guiding this first-time author through the process of publishing a book.

And finally, my family: my wife Tanya, who supported me throughout the book-writing process by carving out the time and space I needed to focus, and my children Boris and Maya, who constantly challenge and inspire me, and who bring me joy when I let myself be present with them.

References

Alexander, Michelle. 2020. *The New Jim Crow: Mass Incarceration in the Age of Colorblindness*. New Press.

Andersen, Maria. 2017. "Write an Operating System for Your Brain". https://busynessgirl.com/write-your-own-personal-operating-system/

Archambeau, Shellye. 2020. *Unapologetically Ambitious: Take Risks, Break Barriers, and Create Success On Your Own Terms*. Grand Central Publishing.

Arkes, H. R., and C. Blumer. 1985. "The Psychology of Sunk Costs." *Organizational Behavior and Human Decision Processes* 35: 124–40.

Berry, Shivani. 2021. "The Best Leaders are Feedback Magnets: Here's How To Become One." https://review.firstround.com/the-best-leaders-are-feedback-magnets-heres-how-to-become-one.

Cain, David. 2019a. "Feel the Air Fully." https://www.raptitude.com/2019/09/feel-the-air-fully/.

Cain, David. 2019b. "How to Make Meditation Ten Times Easier." https://www.raptitude.com/2019/12/how-to-make-meditation-ten-times-easier/.

Carse, James P. 1986. *Finite and Infinite Games*. Ballantine.

Clear, James. 2018. *Atomic Habits*. Penguin Publishing Group.

Cleveland Clinic. 2021. "How Box Breathing Can Help You Destress." August 17, 2021. https://health.clevelandclinic.org/box-breathing-benefits/.

Conscious Leadership Group. n.d. "The 4 Ways of Leading." Accessed August 16, 2023. https://conscious.is/excercises-guides/the-4-ways-of-leading.

Cope, Stephen. 2012. *The Great Work of Your Life: A Guide for the Journey to Your True Calling*. Bantam.

Daisey, Mike. 2002. *21 Dog Years: A Cube-Dweller's Tale.* Free Press.

Dana, Deb. 2023. "Insights from Polyvagal Theory." Coaches Rising podcast, episode 162. February 16, 2023. https://www.coachesrising.com/podcast/insights-from-polyvagal-theory-with-deb-dana/.

Danziger, Shai, Jonathan Levav, and Liora Avnaim-Pesso. 2011. "Extraneous Factors in Judicial Decisions." *Proceedings of the National Academy of Sciences,* April 26, 2011, 108 (17): 6889–92. doi:10.1073/pnas.1018033108.

De Phillips, Frank Anthony, William M. Berliner, and James J. Cribbin. 1960. *Management of Training Programs.* Homewood, IL: Richard D. Irwin.

Dweck, Carol S. 2016. *Mindset: The New Psychology of Success.* Gildan Media Corp.

Eichler, Alex. 2010. "'Askers' vs. 'Guessers'". https://www.theatlantic.com/national/archive/2010/05/askers-vs-guessers/340891/

Ericsson, K. Anders, and William G. Chase. 1982. "Exceptional Memory." *American Scientist* 70, no. 6 (November–December): 607–15.

Ericsson, Anders and Robert Pool. 2016. *Peak: Secrets From the New Science of Expertise.* Houghton Mifflin Harcourt.

Feynman, Richard P. 1985. *Surely You're Joking, Mr. Feynman!: Adventures of a Curious Character.* W.W. Norton.

Fischer, Norman. 2012. *Training in Compassion: Zen Teachings on the Practice of Lojong.* Shambhala.

Fitzpatrick, Rob. 2021. *Write Useful Books: A Modern Approach to Designing and Refining Recommendable Nonfiction.* Useful Books Ltd.

Flores, Fernando. 2012. *Conversations for Action and Collected Essays: Instilling a Culture of Commitment in Working Relationships.* CreateSpace Independent Publishing Platform.

Fogg, BJ. 2020. *Tiny Habits: The Small Changes That Change Everything.* Houghton Mifflin Harcourt.

Frankl, Viktor E. 1946. *Man's Search for Meaning.* Beacon Press.

Gibson, Jeff. 2011. "What Is Your First Team?" The Table Group, Inc., Issue #9, December 2011. https://www.tablegroup.com/thoughts-from-the-field_-issue-9-what-is-your-first-team/.

Goldsmith, Marshall. 2007. *What Got You Here Won't Get You There: How Successful People Become Even More Successful.* Hachette.

Google re:Work. n.d. "Identify Dynamics of Effective Teams." Accessed August 16, 2023. https://rework.withgoogle.com/guides/understanding-team-effectiveness/steps/identify-dynamics-of-effective-teams/.

Goss, Tracy. 2010. *The Last Word On Power: Executive Re-Invention for Leaders Who Must Make the Impossible Happen.* RosettaBooks.

Gottman, John. 1998. *Raising an Emotionally Intelligent Child.* Simon & Schuster.

Haden, Jeff. 2017. "20 Years Ago, Jeff Bezos Said This 1 Thing Separates People Who Achieve Lasting Success From Those Who Don't". https://www.inc.com/jeff-haden/20-years-ago-jeff-bezos-said-this-1-thing-separates-people-who-achieve-lasting-success-from-those-who-dont.html

Hamilton, Arlan, with Nelson, Rachel L. 2020. *It's About Damn Time: How to Turn Being Underestimated into Your Greatest Advantage.* Currency.

Hari, Johann. 2018. *Lost Connections: Uncovering the Real Causes of Depression—and the Unexpected Solutions.* Bloomsbury.

Haslam, S. Alexander, Stephen Reicher, and Michael J. Platow. 2020. *The New Psychology of Leadership: Identity, Influence and Power, 2nd Edition.* Routledge.

Havel, Vaclav. 1985. *The Power of the Powerless.* M.E. Sharpe, Inc.

Hendricks, Kathlyn. 2022. "The Four Pillars of Integrity." The Hendricks Institute. https://hendricks.com/wp-content/uploads/2022/02/Four-Pillars-Two-Page-Document.pdf.

IFS Institute. n.d. "The Internal Family Systems Model Outline." Accessed August 16, 2023. https://ifs-institute.com/resources/articles/internal-family-systems-model-outline.

Kahneman, Daniel. 2011. *Thinking, Fast and Slow.* Farrar, Straus and Giroux.

Kegan, Robert, and Lisa Lahey. 2009. *Immunity to Change: How to Overcome It and Unlock the Potential in Yourself and Your Organization.* Harvard Business Review Press.

Kishimi, Ichiro, and Fumitake Koga. 2018. *The Courage to Be Disliked: The Japanese Phenomenon That Shows You How to Change Your Life and Achieve Real Happiness.* Atria Books.

Leonhardt, David. 2017. "You're Too Busy. You Need A 'Shultz Hour.'" *New York Times.* April 18, 2017. https://www.nytimes.com/2017/04/18/opinion/youre-too-busy-you-need-a-shultz-hour.html.

Levine, Peter A. 1997. *Waking the Tiger: Healing Trauma.* North Atlantic Books.

McKeown, Greg. 2014. *Essentialism: The Disciplined Pursuit of Less.* Crown.

Meadows, Donella H. 2008. *Thinking in Systems: A Primer.* Chelsea Green Publishing.

Merchant, Nilofer. 2017. *The Power of Onlyness: Make Your Wild Ideas Mighty Enough to Dent the World.* Viking.

Mochary, Matt. 2022. "Mochary Method Curriculum." https://docs.google.com/document/d/18FiJbYn53fTtPmphfdCKT2TMWH-8Y2L-MLqDk-MFV4s/edit.

Murthy, Vivek H. 2020. *Together: The Healing Power of Human Connection in a Sometimes Lonely World.* HarperCollins.

Nash, Jennie. 2022. *Blueprint for a Nonfiction Book: Plan and Pitch Your Big Idea.* Tree Farm Books.

Nehrlich, Eric. 2021. "Juneteenth." https://toomanytrees.substack.com/p/juneteenth.

Newport, Cal. 2012. *So Good They Can't Ignore You: Why Skills Trump Passion in the Quest for Work You Love.* Grand Central Publishing.

Novogratz, Jacqueline. 2020. *Manifesto for a Moral Revolution: Practices to Build a Better World.* Henry Holt & Co.

Performance Consultants. n.d. "The GROW Model." Accessed August 16, 2023. https://www.performanceconsultants.com/grow-model.

Real, Terrence. 2022. *Us: Getting Past You & Me to Build a More Loving Relationship.* Goop Press/Rodale.

Robinson, Bryan. 2020. "The 90-Second Rule That Builds Self-Control." *Psychology Today*, April 26, 2020. https://www.psychology-today.com/ca/blog/the-right-mindset/202004/the-90-second-rule-builds-self-control.

Ross, Richard. 1994. "The Ladder of Inference" in *The Fifth Discipline Fieldbook,* edited by Peter Senge, 242–46. Doubleday/Currency.

Saad, Layla M. 2020. *Me and White Supremacy.* Sourcebooks.

Sapolsky, Robert M. 2004. *Why Zebras Don't Get Ulcers.* Times Books.

Senge, Peter M. 1990. *The Fifth Discipline: The Art and Practice of the Learning Organization.* Doubleday/Currency.

Sivers, Derek. 2022. *Anything You Want.* Sivers, Inc. https://sive.rs/a.

Tolentino, Jia. 2016. "On the Origin of Certain Quotable 'African Proverbs'". https://jezebel.com/on-the-origin-of-certain-quotable-african-proverbs-1766664089

Twist, Lynne, with Teresa Barker. 2003. *The Soul of Money: Transforming Your Relationship With Money and Life.* W.W. Norton & Company.

Waitzkin, Josh. 2008. *The Art of Learning: An Inner Journey to Optimal Performance.* Free Press.

Walker, Pete. 2013. *Complex PTSD: From Surviving to Thriving.* Independently published.

Weinberg, Gerald M. 1986. *Becoming a Technical Leader.* Dorset House Publishing.

Yazeed, Carey. 2023. "Black Women and Vulnerability: What Brené Brown Got Wrong." April 5, 2023. https://drcareyyazeed.com/black-women-and-vulnerability-what-brene-brown-got-wrong/.

Additional Resources

Arbinger Institute. 2000. *Leadership and Self-Deception: Getting Out of the Box.* Berrett-Koehler Publishers.

Brown, Brené. 2012. *Daring Greatly: How the Courage to Be Vulnerable Transforms the Way We Live, Love, Parent, and Lead.* Gotham Books.

Cornell, Ann Weiser. 2013. *Focusing on Clinical Practice: The Essence of Change.* W. W. Norton & Company.

Eisler, Riane. 2008. *The Real Wealth of Nations: Creating a Caring Economics.* Berrett-Koehler Publishers.

Horowitz, Ben. 2019. *What You Do Is Who You Are: How to Create Your Business Culture.* New York: Harper Business.

Johnson, Kate. 2021. *Radical Friendship: 7 Ways to Love Yourself and Find Your People in an Unjust World.* Shambhala Publications.

Lebron, Trudi. 2022. *The Antiracist Business Book: An Equity Centered Approach to Work, Wealth, and Leadership.* Row House Publishing.

Lencioni, Patrick. 2012. *The Advantage: Why Organizational Health Trumps Everything Else in Business.* Jossey-Bass.

Nehrlich, Eric. 2020. "Clarity and Focus". https://www.nehrlich.com/blog/2020/11/05/clarity-and-focus/

Scott, Kim. 2019. *Radical Candor: Be a Kick-Ass Boss Without Losing Your Humanity.* St. Martin's Press.

Stone, Douglas, and Bruce Patton and Sheila Heen. 2010. *Difficult Conversations: How to Discuss What Matters Most.* Penguin Books.

About the Author

Eric Nehrlich is an executive coach at www.toomanytrees.com who draws on twenty years of experience in the tech industry to help leaders have more impact. He helps clients gain clarity on their priorities so they can consciously place their focus and attention where they can have the greatest impact. He loves to identify and challenge mindsets and habits that hold his clients back from their next level of leadership. This is Eric's first book, which he wrote to share what he's learned in his career and his coaching with a wider audience.

Before becoming a coach, Eric spent ten years as an engineer and product manager across several startups before joining Google, eventually leading business strategy and operations for the Google Search Ads product team as Chief of Staff for six years.

Eric currently lives in Mountain View, CA with his wife Tanya and their two beautiful children.